OVERTHINKING

Master Your Mind, Eliminate Worries and Negative Thinking While Boosting Your Productivity

EXTENDED VERSION

EMMA CAMPBELL

<u>**YOUR FREE GIFT**</u>

As a way to say thanks, I'm offering you a free workbook exclusively for the readers since I'm convinced that thinking positively can have a dramatic impact on everybody life. Instead of letting negative thoughts like fears, doubts, and anger get in your way, you can embrace calm, confidence, courage, and happiness.

By downloading this workbook "15 ways to think more positive you were not aware of" you will understand how to start thinking more positively with simple exercise in less than 10 minute a day.

Click here to access your free gift or scan the QR code below.

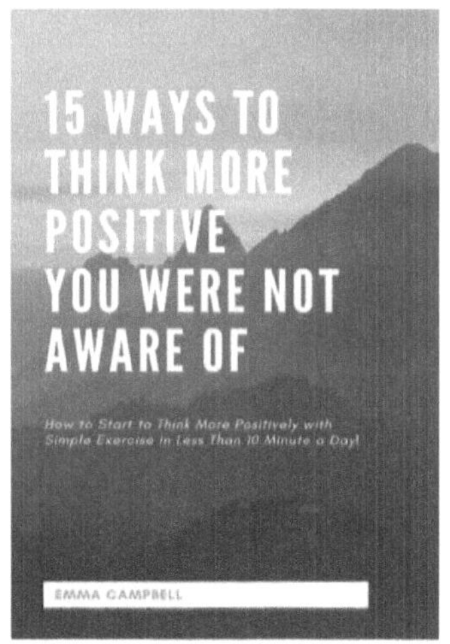

ABSTRACT

Overthinking is an issue that has plagued people of all race, status and culture. In fact, in the aspect of mental health, overthinking can be considered a pandemic. The simple truth is that sometimes, people just tend to think or worry too much, whether consciously or unconsciously. So much so that it begins to interfere with their day to day living, their relationship with other people and in extreme cases, would result to psychological trauma or health problems. So, in the course of this book, we will be looking at understanding the concept of overthinking, why it happens and how to take back your mind from the clutches of worry and stress. At the end of this book, it would be the authors greatest delight that you have gained the necessary information, tools, techniques and skills required to overcome overthinking and by doing so, live a happy, fruitful life.

CHAPTER 1
OVERCOMING OVERTHINKING

What is Overthinking?

Overthinking is actually what it implies, thinking excessively. At the point when you think excessively, rather than acting and getting things done, you are overthinking. At the point when you break down, remark and rehash similar musings over and over, rather than acting, you are overthinking.

This propensity keeps you from making a move. It devours your vitality, cripples your capacity to decide and puts you in a circle of reasoning, thoroughly considering it once more.

This is the sort of reasoning that burns through your time and vitality. It keeps you from acting, doing new things and gaining ground in your life.

It resembles binding yourself with a rope that is tied to a post and then, going around in circles.

In this situation, there is greater probability for worry, anxiety and the absence of internal harmony.

Then again, when you don't overthink, you become increasingly efficient, more peaceful and increasingly cheerful.

What Is Overthinking Disorder?

Do you find yourself overthinking constantly? Are the musings so problematic and inescapable that you have an inclination that your own brain won't just leave you be? Continue reading and realize what this could be.

Overthinking Disorder – what is it?

Overthinking disorder doesn't exist. There is a wide range of anxiety disorders where an individual takes part in overthinking, or rumination, but this is no disorder. At the point when an individual can't quit fixating and stressing over things, it can meddle with your personal satisfaction.

You might be pondering, "What conditions cause overthinking?" Some psychological health diagnosis' where an individual can't prevent their mind from rumination are PTSD, injury, agoraphobia, panic disorder, particular mutism, detachment anxiety, social anxiety, phobias, substance-actuated anxiety, or it might be a side effect of some different ailment.

With regards to anxiety, huge numbers of them have overthinking as an indication. For instance, an individual with panic disorder may ruminate and overthink when they're about to have a panic attack. They fixate on something that could trigger their attack. In addition to the fact they're on edge, they currently have meta-anxiety, which is anxiety about being on edge. Overthinking their fit of anxiety causes them to feel more overwhelmed.

Overthinking is not uncommon. You must not have an anxiety issue that takes part with the consistent rumination. You may state it's a piece of the human condition. We humans tend to overthink things every now and then: You might be excessively worried about what you said or did to someone. You might be stressed over performing at school or work. You may be worried about how others see you. These are large instances of how you may take part in overthinking.

Different instances of overthinking include:

- When you are fixating on what you ought to have said or done
- Performance anxiety, or stressing over how you match up to others at work
- Engaging in "imagine a scenario where" situations which you consider what could occur in an assortment of conditions
- Catastrophizing or thinking the worst will occur
- Worrying about having an unexpected panic attack
- Intrusive or over-the-top thoughts

Overthinking is unavoidable, yet there's hope for the condition. Numerous individuals experience the ill effects of fixating and stressing over things that are out of their control. A typical treatment for this sort of anxiety is Cognitive Behavior Therapy (CBT). CBT assists individuals with testing their negative or nonsensical reasoning and change their thoughts into gainful, positive ones. Getting treatment or counseling for anxiety can have immense effects for somebody with overthinking. You can work with a counselor in your neighborhood, or with one of the prepared mental health experts at Better Help. Online counseling is an excellent place to deal with anxiety and begin to learn coping mechanisms to manage it.

Numerous individuals know about the term anxiety disorder (and, in fact, many Americans experience the ill effects of a type of anxiety issue each day), yet we will ignore a significant side effect of anxiety, which is from overthinking.

The meaning of overthinking is to ruminate or fixate on something. Many individuals, when hearing this definition, may accept they are overthinkers. Who doesn't go a single day without overthinking something? We wonder if we're settling on the correct decisions from little things like picking the quickest course on our drive that morning, or choosing the correct eatery for supper to things like our kids' prosperity, and our family's health and security. Be that as it may, that is typical. It's entirely expected to stress and overthink to some extent.

But there are still destructive impacts overthinking can have on an individual intellectually and inwardly. While overthinking in accordance with an anxiety disorder, it would be unnecessary to contemplation about something that causes one tension, stress, dread, or fear. It's not simply just pondering about something; it's fixating on something so much that it influences one's capacity to work in their life. At the point where you wonder or stress over yourself, your life, your family, your companions, or whatever else and you don't have an overthinking issue, whatever you're contemplating about only stresses you for some time, and after a brief time frame, you go on with your day. You keep stressing now and again, however, you don't continually ruminate. You don't discover the stress meddling with the rest of your life. With overthinking as the consequence of an anxiety disorder, the stress is all the individual can consider and despite the fact they may not fixate on something very similar constantly, they're always worried about something.

On the off chance that you believe you may experience the ill effects of overthinking because of anxiety, you may have discovered that you've encountered at least one of these circumstances:

- Difficulty tracking and adding to a discussion since you go over potential reactions or explanations until the discussion has either finished or the fateful opening for talking was lost
- Continually contrasting yourself with the individuals around you and how you measure up
- Focusing on the most pessimistic scenarios either involving yourself or the ones you love
- Reliving past disappointments or slip-ups again and again until you can't move past them
- Worrying about future errands as well as objectives until they feel practically difficult to achieve
- Reliving a past horrible encounter, (for example, abuse or the passing of a friend or family member) leaving you incapable to adapt to it
- A powerlessness to hinder the obscure contemplations, stresses or feelings racing through your mind

No two individuals will encounter overthinking the same way. In any case, the individuals who do encounter it will all find that their personal satisfaction is undermined by their powerlessness to adequately control pessimistic thoughts and feelings. This can make it increasingly hard to go out and mingle, appreciate interests, or be effective at work as their mind invests a lopsided measure of time and vitality on explicit lines of thought. There's a feeling that they don't have full authority over their own personalities or feelings, which can be harming to one's mental health.

Making friends or just keeping them can also be troublesome with overthinking where you may find it difficult to communicate when something isn't right or you may convey too much. It tends to be amazingly hard to converse with them since you're worried about what to state or do anything with them since you're excessively worried about how you'll do or what will occur. Somebody who overthinks may battle even to continue general discussions or to interface in a typical domain. They may experience anxiety even with small tasks such as heading off to the store or even to meet up with someone.

In all actuality, overthinking can influence everything without exception about your life. It can influence the way you work with others, sway your public activity, and negatively affect your own life. This means it can begin to erode at you and at the connections you have with the individuals around you. Overthinking can make major issues throughout your life.

Two Forms of Overthinking

Overthinking comes in two structures; ruminating about the past and worrying over what's to come.

It's not quite the same as critical thinking. Critical thinking includes contemplating an answer. Overthinking involving harping on about the issue.

Overthinking is not quite the same as self-reflection. Solid self-reflection involves getting to discover something new about oneself or increasing another viewpoint about a circumstance. It's deliberate.

Overthinking includes harping on about how awful you feel and worrying about all the things you have no control or influence over. It won't assist you with growing new knowledge.

The distinction between critical thinking, self-reflection, and overthinking isn't about the measure of time you spend on the profound idea. Time spent creating innovative solutions or gaining from your conduct is profitable. Be that as it may, time spent overthinking, regardless of whether its 10 minutes or 10 hours, won't upgrade your life.

At the point when you become increasingly mindful of your inclination to overthink things, you can find a way to change. Above all, you need to understand that overthinking accomplishes more mischief than anything.

Here and there, individuals imagine their overthinking keeps terrible things from occurring. Also, they think in the event that if they don't stress enough or repeat the past enough, at some point at one way or another, they'll experience more issues. However, the exploration is quite clear; overthinking is awful for you and it does nothing to forestall or take mindfulness of issues.

Bipolar Disorder and Overthinking

At the point when one considers bipolar disorder, they will in generally think of the psychological health information they know about. Furthermore, that health information is the way that bipolar individuals will either be depressed or hyperactive. Individuals with this condition will have a hard time with their state of mind, however, they may also have a hard time with overthinking.

With bipolar disorder, overthinking, upsetting, or troubling thoughts can occur with the two sides of the coin. With depression, one might be stressed over what will occur later on. Or, on the other hand, they may stress over the effects of the medicine they take.

With lunacy, you may experience difficulty focusing on your musings, making it harder to challenge your thoughts. It's difficult to separate the genuine from the fiction. Or then again, you might be so euphoric you invest energy spending to gain a sense of security, but at that point you think twice about it.

With bipolar disorder, it's significant you look for the assistance of online treatment or an in-person advisor. Online treatment works particularly well for mellow to moderate cases. An advisor can give you the fundamental information and mental health information about bipolar disorder. Furthermore, it's significant you focus on your thoughts.

In some cases, your bipolar fits can keep going for various time frames, and your thoughts can compound them. You may concentrate on the negative and cause your disorder to compound for extensive stretches of time. If you have bipolar disorder or not, your thoughts that fly into your psyche will aggravate the issue. Look for help if you need it.

About Mentally Strong People

Intellectually resilient individuals are a class of people that are more averse to overthink. Think about your mind as a muscle. The more you train it, the more intellectually solid you'll get. Expanding your psychological health strength is particularly significant as you age. Mental health decreases with maturing, yet with the correct health information, you can work on your mind.

Here is some acceptable mental health information for your mind:

1. Mentally resilient individuals exercise a great deal:

At the point when you consider work out, you may envision resilient individuals improving your body. In any case, practice has numerous positive symptoms for your mind. For instance, your brain discharges feel-good signals that kill pain and help lessen your stress hormones. Also, practice occupies you from your thoughts, making it extraordinary in the event that you need to know how to quit overthinking.

2. Mentally tough individuals attempt to associate as much as they can:

Have a go at conversing with a dear companion and contact them on a more profound level. In the event that you don't have any companions to converse with, take a stab at getting out and conversing with somebody in a book shop, cafe, or anywhere else. At the point when you're conversing with new individuals and attempting to make friends, you're encountering substantially less stress while being more up to date.

3. Intellectually resilient individuals consistently practice cognitive behavioral therapy:

This kind of therapy causes you to dispose of unfortunate propensities and thoughts, and it tends to be utilized to treat a wide range of psychological illness, dietary issues, bipolar disorder, summed up anxiety issue, and a lot more.

4. Strong individuals will train themselves intellectually by blending it up:

Doing similar things again and again can have some negative symptoms. Take a look at a part of your life and think of what you can do any other way. Take a stab at having another pastime, going for your dream job, or simply discovering some new information. At the point when you begin living for another day, it assists with your overthinking.

5. Strong individuals will understand that there will be seasons of shortcoming:

There are times where you invest a lot of energy thinking, and afterward you notice yourself overthinking. It will occur, and you can't overthink this, however, it occurs. Simply don't go through hours on it. You can plan an opportunity to let your mind meander about a particular issue, and when that time is up, quit pondering it. This is something that may take practice, however, resilient individuals can give it a shot.

The Most Effective Method to Decrease Mental Stress

Here's a little break in transmission if may ask why "decrease mental stress" is on here. All things considered, stress and our propensity to overthink are intertwined. Stress is our body's approach to help us when we're up the creek without a paddle in a circumstance that undermines us. In any case, our body can't differentiate between genuine danger and normal issues, and accordingly the stress heaps on. People think that it's difficult to adapt to all their stress.

Some stress can be acceptable. Stress related with positive psychological science, which is acceptable stress, will test you and make you need to improve. But in any case, positive psychological research can only go so far. A lot of stress can exacerbate your issues, including: making you dread rejection, blame, disappointment, or losing everything.

Stress happens to everyone alike. It doesn't make a difference in case you're a kid, in your teenager years, or an adult. In the event that you have a propensity for overthinking and have worry, here are some straightforward approaches to lessen stress. Anybody can do these straightforward procedures, and these basic procedures don't require a specialist, either.

1. Practice cognitive behavioral therapy: This is something that takes practice, yet figuring out how to distinguish thoughts are, by definition, meddlesome, and figuring out how to adapt to these thoughts is significant.

2. Write down your issues and organize them from most to least important: A part of critical thinking includes you taking mindfulness of the simplest issue first and proceeding upward. Before long, you'll discover problem solving won't be so difficult.

3. Think of your fear of disappointment and other regular fears: Why do you dread this? How does your stress affect you? Do you fear guilt, disappointment, or something else?

4. People don't understand the benefit of working out. It can help diminish your worry by a considerable amount.

5. Take opportunities to loosen up: See what's going on with your preferred show. Try not to invest a lot of energy stalling, however, enjoy a reprieve and return with a crisp mind.

6. Don't ingest medications or liquor: If conversing with an advisor or therapist drives them to endorse medicine, take that.

Lastly, take a stab at working with a counselor. They might be able to assist you with your issues.

7. Hypochondria: This is another condition where you generally feel you have something restoratively amiss with anxiety, and it becomes a major issue with overthinking.

There are a few people who are somewhat hypochondriac. For example, you may think something isn't right with you. After visiting Dr. Google, you converse with your primary physician. At that point, you find that nothing is wrong and it's only an issue with overthinking, blended in with an anxiety issue.

You might be an extreme hypochondriac if you're continually meeting with your primary physician about something. After you converse with your primary physician, despite having those feelings, no measure of conversation with your PCP will cause them to leave. Regardless of how much you argue the point, you believe you're sick.

This is something you have to look for help with. You may have something other than a small anxiety issue. By getting treatment, you can gather the mental fortitude to say that you're fine.

8. Seek Motivation: While numerous individuals are doubtful about an inspirational orator, they might have the option to help. Perusing tales about a man who had the option to beat anxiety and live, or individuals who figured out how to begin living at a more seasoned age, can move you and is a decent method to occupy you from your overthinking.

It's a decent method to get some psychological health information at an individual level. While a portion of this mental health information may not be a piece of contemporary brain science, there is some merit into looking at it.

For instance, therapist and creator Eckhart Tolle is a good place to go for health information. "Profound therapist and creator Eckhart Tolle?" you inquire. Eckhart Tolle has composed numerous books about the present time and place, which what health information about abstaining from overthinking is about.

9. When it comes to care, read all the health information you can get. A few books are short and don't set aside a great deal of effort to peruse. Others do take a great deal of time, however, the information they give isn't justified, despite all the trouble. Some self-improvement guides sound somewhat mushy, however, you'll be shocked with the amount it can help with recuperating, rejection, blame, disappointment, and different issues.

With regards to overthinking, it's fundamental to devour all the mindfulness content you can. Mindfulness is the way to getting the assistance you need.

10. Something Else?

It merits referencing that how we think and how the mind functions are a riddle. There are numerous clinical preliminaries, both clinical, social, and in the past, that may show us more of the psyche. In any case, these clinical preliminaries are only that, clinical, social, and mental preliminaries.

It's possible that one day we will have a pill for fixing overthinking, however, that day is quite a while away.

Overthinking is a conduct that could happen whenever. For somebody who has anxiety or any kind of anxiety disorder, it can have the indication of overthinking, too. The tension and the stress that you have over various circumstances and various obstructions throughout your life can rapidly transform into overthinking and pondering about what you ought to do or how you could prevent terrible things from occurring. In all actuality, you can't prevent every single awful thing from occurring and you can't prevent yourself from each terrible choice. However, what you can do is find support.

If you've been battling to quit from overthinking, it might be useful to look for professional treatment. You can discover help from multiple points of view, however, an advantageous and private spot to begin is by means of an Internet advising webpage like BetterHelp.com. There, you will discover access to authorized instructors prepared to assist you with conquering your battles with overthinking. You don't need to stop your thoughts all on your own. Trust an online specialist to manage you toward a more advantageous perspective about your life, and carrying on with your life consistently.

With online treatment, you'll have the option to speak with an authorized, private mental health supplier without agonizing over being send off to an office, or in any event, being seen by anybody except the counselor's themselves. You can feel increasingly great since you're in a setting that makes you feel best in; your home. You'll have command over what's happening, too. The entirety of this can make it simpler for you to open up and for you to begin your mending journey with your therapist. You should simply locate the right one.

Activities to improve your psychological strength: Whether you're enticed to avoid the gym since you don't want to get off the love seat, or you're addressing whether you were removed to be a business visionary, it is difficult to summon the psychological strength you require to arrive at your objectives.

In any case, before you fault, you're not nullifying your absence of natural determination. Think about this; it takes a couple of moments to begin fabricating the psychological will you need to arrive at your most prominent potential.

Building mental strength could be likened to building physical strength. Doing 50 push-ups a day would just take a couple of moments of your time. However, on the off chance that you did it each and every day, you'd build up some great chest muscle strength.

The equivalent can be said with your psychological muscle. It only takes a couple of moments of every day to prepare your mind to think in an unexpected way. With predictable exercise, you'll fabricate the psychological strength you need to deal with your feelings.

How to Tell You're an Overthinker?

You can't quit thinking about an occasion, an individual, something that previously occurred, or on an issue. Rather than searching for an answer, stepping up to the plate and being dynamic, you simply continue thinking and slowly drift to the verge of insanity.

On occasion, when something awful occurs, you consider the most exceedingly terrible situations with contemplations like "imagine a scenario in which?" or "why?"

You sometimes slip into negative reasoning examples:

- You stress over past slip-ups or current issues and obstacles, and how they may prompt negative result
- You fixate on or over-break downs with your everyday encounters and cooperation with individuals
- You expand each word, thought and occasion past its extreme and sensible extents, adding something extra to it, things that aren't really there

In the event this happens regularly, you are what psychologists call an overthinker or a ruminator.

Psychologists have discovered that overthinking can hinder productivity and lead to anxiety and sorrow.

In spite of the fact that some proof recommends ladies are bound to be overthinkers more than men, in all actuality, everybody overthinks every now and again.

The connection between overthinking and mental health issues is a chicken-or-egg type question. Overthinking is connected to mental issues, similar to depression and anxiety.

Almost certainly, overthinking makes mental health decline, and as your psychological health decreases, the more probable you are to overthink. It's an awful, descending spiral.

In any case, it's difficult to perceive that spiral when you're trapped in the middle of it. Truth be told, your brain might attempt to persuade you that stressing and ruminating is helping in some way or another.

All things considered, won't you build up a superior arrangement or keep yourself from committing a similar error where you invest more energy into thinking? Not really.

The inverse is frequently valid. Analysis paralysis is a genuine issue. The more you think, the more regrettable you feel. Furthermore, your sentiments of wretchedness, anxiety, or outrage may cloud your judgment and keep you from making positive moves.

So below, we will also be taking a look at 15 clear signs that you're an over-thinker, even if it doesn't seem that way to you.

You've presumably been informed that the world was at your feet. You have more options than any other time in recent memory and you should be fortunate there are bounteous open doors out there.

This thought can be a gift for a few, but not so much for others.

If you're an over-thinker like me, it tends to be debilitating going through each conceivable situation for each potential chance.

The uncertainties begin to run your life and you can get so consumed that you can forget what your initial intention was.

It's much more dreadful when you don't know you're doing it!

1. You see things that aren't there

Somebody you like spins their hair twice, rather than multiple times. You stroll past somebody and they don't look at you, yet you stroll past them again and this time they look for two or three seconds. They turned away excessively quick. What does everything mean!? When you're an over-thinker, you will need to discover significance in your general surroundings. Here and there, it can devour you while you over-dissect everything. It's helpful to advise yourself that nothing has innate importance other than the significance you give it.

2. You think more than you do

Ever heard the term analysis paralysis? You suspect as much that you don't wind up busy. You gauge your alternatives. You conclude what the best result might be, however, you contrast the best result and another conceivable best result. The cycle proceeds until you wind up sitting idle. Rather than considering each chance, you think it's accommodating to really begin trying out some of the results to check whether they are actually evident.

3. You get energized when you've at long last made sense of something

Perhaps you've been pondering something over for a considerable length of time. A complex problem that you haven't made sense of yet, however, you kept at it. Or, on the other hand, a mind-boggling love intrigue that you've fixated on until they accomplish something that demonstrates your whole hypothesis about them. In any case, you bounce for happiness shouting, "Eureka!" when you've at long last made sense of the appropriate response. At that point, you move onto your next issue and even start to address whether you really made sense of the first issue.

4. You think that it's hard to let things go

Since you've put in a ton of exertion into making sense of something, you think that it's difficult to relinquish. You effectively connect to things you find significant. You don't need to fall flat. When you've contributed a ton of time and energy into something, it very well may be difficult to release it when it isn't working. You may keep contemplating it considerably, even after you believe you previously let it go. The more you consider something, the more it can harm you.

5. You show restraint

You notice the amount of time it takes to dot your i's and cross your t's. Regardless of whether it takes you longer than most, you are pleased when you win the competition because you've put in the effort to make sense of it. You're willing to sit on the information you've acquired till you feel comfortable, regardless of others seeking more immediate solutions.

6. You need to get the entirety of your affairs in order

Be cautious with this one. This can frequently be a reason not to make a move. While you think that it's soothing to hold up until you feel prepared, you may never feel prepared and may just postpone the inescapable. I know this since I used to state this. Now and again, there will never be a best time and you will never have as much time as you do now. You might as well go into the water and then sort out your affairs.

7. You are continually looking for new information

A companion gives you an article about a topic you're keen on. You get a notice from Facebook that you were tagged in a photograph and at the same time, you receive a text from somebody asking something of you. At that point, your work friend stands up and needs to try this new café for lunch. With such a large number of interruptions, there is an inclination to know more information.

8. You need to know the why

Children love to inquire as to why. It's hot out today. Why? Don't converse with outsiders. Why? Walk don't run. Why? Overthinkers will keep this internal identity with them for a long duration. They aren't intrigued by such a great amount in surface level importance, yet the why is behind it. This can be amazingly helpful in taking mindfulness of complex issues, having profound discussions, and contemplating the significance of life. At times it may very well be impeding, in light of the fact that a few things DO have surface level significance. We need effortlessness, yet we make things complex.

9. You need to get everything right

You may be a fussbudget, but from one's perspective, you highly esteem yourself at being extraordinary at what you do and endeavor to give a valiant effort. When you don't get everything right and miss the mark, you can turn into your own harshest critic. By perceiving this, it can be a quality just as a shortcoming, however, you can ease up a bit by realizing that you basically can't get everything right, in spite of your earnest attempts. Give yourself some breathing space.

10. You fear a single word answer

When you ask somebody how they are doing? And all you get is good, you wince a tad. There is significantly more to that question than great. Needing to know more, you may pry somewhat more and pose more inquiries since you need to make sense of how they really are. How great? Great or only somewhat great? Great today? Great at this moment? While you might have the option to continue forever about how you're feeling, you may expect every other person to do the same.

11. You accept others recognize what you're thinking

Those voices in your head are uproarious to you, however, you may overlook that they are yours and yours alone. You may get calm and expect another person will know precisely what is happening in that head of yours. In any case, in the event that you don't impart it, others won't know. While you may incline toward calm situations, you begin to understand that your overthinking gets stronger when there aren't the same number of interruptions. You may notice that internal identity coming out again when you don't get your way.

12. You are an admirer of records

The delight of making a huge rundown and intersection out of those things as you complete them is exceptionally rousing. At the point when you attempt and offer your adoration for records with others, they may not revel in that equivalent satisfaction. In any case, you keep on making them! The fulfillment of arranging something and outwardly observing all that arranging getting checked off is pleasurable.

13. You anticipate getting things done to quiet the psyche

Long strolls. Reflection. Composing. Exercise. A conversation. You appreciate doing things that remove your brain from your overthinking mode. While your psyche is dynamic, you think that it's hard and you have the inclination to accomplish more. It's supportive to advise yourself that you are a person and not a human doing. This will permit your brain to take a much-merited break.

14. You break down individuals

This incorporates yourself! You may ask why individuals do the things they do. You appreciate people viewing since you need to attempt to make sense of them. Open spots can be both interesting and overpowering to you. To you, somebody just doesn't stroll by. You may have watched the manner they walked with or pondered what melody they're listening to. On the off chance that somebody is conversing with themselves, you may need to advise yourself that they are conversing with themselves and not you. At that point you wonder why they are conversing with themselves in the first place.

15. You think fundamentally

At times you see elective answers for complex issues. Perhaps you have a few thoughts that no one has ever thought of previously. Once in a while you can sit and gaze off in amazement at the multifaceted nature of life. Simple answers aren't sufficient to you. You need to go further. You gauge the entirety of your choices, cautiously researching further. Your capacity to think is a quality you are profoundly pleased with.

A portion of our most noteworthy creators, visionaries, business visionaries, and thought pioneers were all masterminds. It can be extremely constraining and even forlorn now and again.

When you can see both the qualities and constraints of your overthinking, you can adjust your degree of overthinking with more doing. You can even show another person who underthinks!

Take comfort knowing you aren't the only one who overthinks and recollects these 15 signs that make you presumable you are a mastermind, regardless of whether you don't feel like one.

However, don't consider it to an extreme.

What Happens to Your Body When You Overthink?

In the event that you go over past discussions, harp on about something during your decisions or get caught in a passage of "consider the possibility that" situations, there's a decent possibility that you're an overthinker.

This broad rumination and over-fixating has, to some degree, become a pestilence. One examination from the University of Michigan found that 73% of adults between the ages of 25 and 35 overthink, as do 52% of 45to 55-year-olds.

Numerous overthinkers accept they're really helping themselves out by burning through their musings. Yet, the reality of the situation is that overthinking is a perilous game that can have a great deal of negative results on our prosperity.

As David Spiegel, the Executive of the Center on worry and Health at Stanford Health Care, puts it, "There are times when the stress over the issue is a great deal more terrible than the issue itself."

This is what happens to your body when you overthink:

1. You're less inclined to make a move:

Overthinking makes such a significant number of choices, decisions and situations that makes you end up being unfit to settle on a choice.

"You could stall out in potential results that may not by any means occur, simply agonizing over specific results, and that can deaden us or freeze us from making a move," said Rajita Sinha, the chief of the Yale Stress Center.

When you do push ahead with a choice, you may end up making an inappropriate one since you got so stirred up by all the contending thoughts.

"Your premonition or impulse gets superseded in light of the fact that you have so a lot other information ... and you possibly end up not settling on the decisions that are directly for you at that time," said Laura Price, a clinical partner teacher in the division of psychiatry at NYU Langone Health.

2. You're less innovative:

An investigation from the U.K. found that when certain pieces of your mind and psychological procedures hush up, you're progressively imaginative. Overthinking — which can prompt a "psychological groove," as the examination notes mention — can basically make you stall out and come up short on thoughts or new arrangements. While some overthinking can prompt crisp, new thoughts, it can also reverse discharge and make mental detours that make you try to consider some fresh possibilities.

Another investigation from Stanford arrived at a similar resolution. While snared to attractive reverberation imaging machines, members were solicited to draw an arrangement from pictures — some simple to outline, some troublesome. The more troublesome the pictures were to draw, the more the members needed to think, and the less innovative their drawings were. On the other side, the less the idea included, the more inventive the drawings were.

So, an excess of speculation appeared to set a limit for imagination.

3. Your vitality levels may drop:

It takes a ton of mental vitality to overthink. Your mind is creating such a large number of various contemplations and situations that aren't generally going toward anything beneficial.

"Mental vitality with no kind of physical outlet totally can cause it exhausting and cause it to feel like you're depleted in light of the fact that you invested such a great amount of energy in your own head," Price said.

Spiegel included that when we overthink and worry ourselves, our bodies produce cortisol, the stress hormone. After some time, that consistent arrival of cortisol can be draining and cause burnout.

"It resembles running your vehicle in an inappropriate rigging. Your engine's running however you're not getting much of anywhere," Spiegel said.

4. Your rest may endure a shot:

Bunches of overthinkers' battle with nodding off, rearranging through contemplations instead of closing down and hitting the hay.

Your body needs to get into a condition of quiet so you can rest — your pulse needs to go down, as does your circulatory strain and relaxing. Overanalyzing can be stimulating, particularly when the musings are progressively on edge. This can haul you out of the alleviating state your body should be in for rest.

Furthermore, when your rest begins enduring, it's anything but difficult to stall out in a frightful tornado of depletion and lack of sleep.

"On the off chance that you don't rest also, you have less vitality, you get less exercise, at that point you rest much more dreadful," Spiegel said.

5. Your craving may change:

Overthinking can profoundly affect individuals' cravings. For a few, it can stifle hunger, and for other people it can help it — which is progressively normal.

Spiegel calls this "stress eating," and said individuals do this since it tends to divert, or in any event, mitigate it. "Numerous individuals will go for the most delectable and unhealthiest things when they're focused on," Spiegel stated, taking note of how "there's an explanation for high-fat and sugary nourishments that are classified 'comfort food sources.'"

Furthermore, cortisol — that stress hormone we discussed before — expands your craving alongside your inspiration to eat, as indicated by Harvard University.

Here's the manner to control your inclination to overthink.

The initial step is to see that you're overthinking and get mindful of what's happening. As indicated by Sinha, one approach to consider is that you have excess of three potential, or "imagine a scenario," situations that you're contemplating it to an extreme.

Next, you need to figure out how to divert yourself and get into your physical body to let loose of your subjective frameworks (think going for a run or attempting yoga). Value rehearses, diaphragmatic breathing, or profound tummy breathing can help bring down your pulse, slow your breathing, and connect with your body — which clears your head.

She also suggested utilizing a stress log: 20 minutes before bed, record a rundown of everything that you're agonizing over or need to do.

"The way toward recording it — not composing, however composing — has a preparing impact to your brain to help get it out of that turn cycle," Price said.

Conversing with an advisor, companion or cherished one can give you a crisp point of view and understand that something appears to be horrible or complex isn't so convoluted.

In conclusion, mindfulness or contemplation can assist you with resetting and cleaning up your brain, however, this will probably take a touch of training and persistence.

"Try not to battle the issue — let it course through you like watching the tempest cruise by," he said.

CHAPTER 2
MASTERY OF THE MIND

Freud's Model of the Human Mind

Understanding the human brain is at the center of psychoanalytic hypothesis. Since the presentation of the hypothesis of Sigmund Freud in the mid 1900s, and in spite of the numerous headways in the investigation of psychoanalytic hypothesis, Freud's essential contemplations hold a solid hang on the molding of perspectives in regards to the hypothesis of the human brain.

At the focal point of Freud's hypothesis are psychopathologies that bring about a dysfunctional behavior inside a subject. It is Freud's reason that contained within the human mind there is three degrees of mindfulness or awareness. It is the presentation of these psychopathologies that influence individuals in this manner, which requires more than a basic discussion. The successful treatment of these profound situated psychopathologies is called therapy.

In the representation underneath is Freud's division of these three levels and the evaluated utilization of each level. They are the cognizant, intuitive, and oblivious. Cooperating with them makes us know our perceived world.

Despite the fact that acknowledgment of Freud's psychoanalytical hypothesis has ebbed and streamed after some time not many experts would propose excusing it. Inside it is a model or idea that has withstood the numerous trials of time.

Etymology

The inception of the significance of the mind offers a long and rich history. Like all numerous different words and expressions there is no unmistakable development given for its utilization. Its importance was increasingly reliant on the setting of its use as opposed to any single significance.

Whenever talked about by a rationalist the brain may well mean one's character, personality, and their recollections. For the strict the brain houses the soul, a consciousness of God, or to the researcher the mind is the generator of thoughts. In its early stages references to the mind genuinely were allegorical.

It wasn't until the fourteenth and fifteenth century that the speculation of the mind to incorporate every intellectual capacity, thought, volition, feeling, and memory bit by bit was created.

In the late nineteenth and mid-twentieth century brain research became the front line in science due to no little part crafted by Freud and others, the mainstream center around the human psyche, its job in the conduct sciences, and the brain/body question set. Today, the idea of the mind and its capacities is quite often examined from a logical perspective.

Freud's Categories of the Mind

- Freud's conscious mind
- Freud's subconscious mind

- Freud's unconscious mind

Freud's Conscious Mind

Since cognizance is best comprehended as having a consciousness of something, having the option to bring it to mind, it would appear to be sufficiently straightforward to qualify just those occasions we can review as the exercises of the human psyche.

There are two difficulties to this view. To start with, there is the gauge that just about 10% of the psyches work is comprised of cognizant idea and besides, this view doesn't clarify those irregular occasions made inside the brain.

The two capacities and abilities of the cognizant brain can address are:

1) Its capacity to coordinate your core interest

2) Its capacity to envision what can't

While a significant accomplice in the group of three of the human brain, the cognizant mind fills in as a scanner for us. It will see an occasion, trigger a need to respond, and afterward relying upon the significance of the occasion, and store it either in the oblivious or the subliminal territory of the human mind where it stays accessible to us.

Freud's Subconscious Mind

Your intuitive is the capacity point for any ongoing recollections required for snappy review, for example, what your phone number is or the name of an individual you just met. It additionally holds current information that you utilize each day, like your current repeating contemplations, personal conduct standards, propensities, and sentiments.

The workhorse of the psyche/body experience of Freud's intuitive brain fills in as the personality's arbitrary access memory (RAM). "In this manner the oblivious mind can be viewed as the wellspring of dreams and programmed musings (those that show up with no obvious reason), the store of overlooked recollections (that may at present be open to awareness at some later time), and the locus of understood information (The things that we have adapted so well that we do them without speculation)."

Freud's Unconscious Mind

The oblivious mind is the place the entirety of our recollections and past encounters live. These are those recollections that have been curbed through injury and those that have basically been intentionally overlooked and are no longer essential to us (programmed musings). It's from these recollections and encounters that our convictions, propensities, and practices are framed.

An audit of the prior outline shows the oblivious, sitting a layer further in the brain under the intuitive. In spite of the fact that the intuitive and oblivious has direct connects to one another and manage comparable things, the oblivious brain is actually the basement, the underground library of every one of your recollections, propensities, and practices. It is the storage facility of all your profound situated feelings that have been customized since birth.

Freud's psychoanalytic hypothesis encourages that it is here, in the oblivious brain that essential change can happen by using therapy.

The Most Effective Method to Control Your Thoughts and Be the Master of Your Mind

Let me reiterate. Your mind is the most amazing asset you have for the production of good in your life, however, if it's not utilized properly, it can be the most damaging force in your life.

Your brain, all the more explicitly, your musings, influence your recognition and your understanding of the real world.

I have heard that the average individual thinks around 70,000 thoughts every day. That is a lot, particularly in the event that they are useless, self-damaging, and only a general misuse of vitality.

You can let your thoughts go crazy, but for what reason would you? It is your brain, your musings; isn't it an opportunity to take your capacity back? Isn't it an opportunity to take control?

Decide to be the individual who is effectively, deliberately thinking about your musings. Become the ace of your brain.

At the point when you change your thoughts, you will change your emotions too, and you will also dispose of the triggers that set off those sentiments. Both of these results furnish you with a more prominent degree of harmony in your brain.

As of now, I have barely any contemplations that are not based on my very own preference or a reaction from my reinventing. I am the ace of my brain, so now my mind is very quiet. Yours can be as well!

"Who Is Thinking My Thoughts?"

Before you can turn into the maestro of your psyche, you should perceive that you are helpless before a few undesirable "squatters" living in your brain, and they are accountable for your musings. If you need to be the manager of them, you should know what their identity is and what their inspiration is, and afterward you can assume responsibility and oust them.

Here are four of the "squatters" in your mind that make the most unfortunate and ineffective contemplations:

1. **The Inner Critic**

This is your steady abuser who is regularly a mixture of:

Others' words; ordinarily your folks, contemplations you have made dependent on your own or different people groups desires, contrasting yourself with others, incorporating those in the media.

The things you let yourself know because of agonizing encounters, for example, are disloyalty and dismissal. Your understanding makes your self-uncertainty and self-fault, which are probably undeserved in instances of dismissal and selling out.

The Inner Critic is roused by torment, low confidence, absence of self-acknowledgment, and absence of self-esteem.

For what other reason would this individual maltreatment do for you? What's more, since this person is really you — why else would you misuse yourself? For what reason would you let anybody treat you this severely?

2. **The Worrier**

This individual lives later on in the realm of "what worries."

The Worrier is roused by dread which is frequently silly and there's no reason for it. Infrequently, this individual is roused by dread that what occurred in the past will happen once more.

3. **The Reactor or Trouble-Maker**

This is the one that triggers outrage, dissatisfaction, and agony. These come from unhealed injuries of the past. Any experience that is even firmly identified with a past injury will set this individual off.

This individual can be set off by words or emotions, and can even be set off by sounds and scents.

The Reactor has no genuine inspiration, has poor motivation control, and is controlled by past programming that never again serves you, in the event that it could possibly do so.

4. **The Sleep Depriver**

This can be a blend of any number of various squatters, including the internal organizer, the rehashed, and the ruminator alongside the inner critic and the worrier.

The Sleep Depriver's inspiration can be: as a response to quietness, which will the individual fight against?

Dealing with the business you neglected during the day, self-question, low confidence, uncertainty and anxiety add to the mix.

As recorded above for the inward pundit and worrier, how might you control these squatters?

Step by Step Instructions to Master Your Mind

You are the thinker and the onlooker of your thoughts. You should focus on your thoughts so you can recognize "who" is managing everything. This will:

Figure out which method you need to utilize

Start every day with the aim of focusing on your musings and getting yourself when you are thinking bothersome thoughts

These are two different ways to control your thoughts:

Technique A – Interrupt and supplant them

Technique B – Eliminate them entirely

This subsequent choice is what is known as genuine feelings of serenity!

The system of hindering and supplanting is a method for reinventing your intuitive psyche. In the end, the substitution thoughts will turn into the "go to" musings in the appropriate circumstances.

Use Technique A with the Inner Critic and Worrier; and Technique B with the Reactor and Sleep Depriver.

1. For the Inner Critic

At the point when you discover yourself contemplating something negative about yourself (calling yourself names, slighting yourself, or censuring yourself), interfere with it.

You can holler (in your brain), "Stop! No!" or "Enough! I'm in charge now." Then, whatever your negative idea was about yourself, supplant it with an inverse, counter idea, or an attestation that starts with "I am."

For instance, if your idea is, "I'm such a failure," you can supplant it with, "I am a Divine Creation of the Universal Spirit. I am an ideal profound being figuring out how to ace the human experience. I am a being of vitality, light, and matter. I am heavenly, splendid, and lovely. I love and endorse myself similarly as I am."

You can also have a discourse with yourself with the goal of ruining the "voice" that made the idea, the one you know whose voice it is.

"Because someone said I was a failure doesn't make it genuine. It was their supposition, not an announcement of reality. Or then again perhaps they were kidding and I paid attention to it since I'm uncertain."

In the event that you perceive you've been repeating self-basic contemplations, you can work out or pre-plan your counter thoughts or attestation so you can be prepared. This is the primary squatter you ought to oust, strongly, if essential.

They provoke the Worrier. The names you call yourself become triggers when called those names by others, so the individual keeps up with the nearness of the Reactor.

They are frequently present when you attempt to nod off so he sustains the Sleep Depriver.

They are a harasser and is loudly and genuinely damaging.

They simply destroy your self-esteem. They persuade you that you're not commendable. They're a liar! In light of a legitimate concern for your self-esteem, get them out!

Dispense with your most exceedingly awful pundit and you will also decrease the nearness of the other three squatters.

Supplant them with your new closest companions who support, empower, and upgrade your life. This is a nearness you need in your brain.

2. For the Worrier

Drawn out anxiety is intellectually, sincerely, and genuinely undesirable. It can have long haul health effects.

Dread starts the battle of fight-or-flight reaction, making stress in the brain and raises anxiety in the body.

You ought to have the option to perceive a "stress thought" quickly by how you feel. The physiological signs that the battle or flight reaction of dread has kicked in are: blood pressure, heart rate increase, or flood of adrenaline, shallow breathing or breathlessness, and tense muscles.

Utilize the above expressed technique to interfere with any idea of stress and afterward replace it. In any case, this time you will supplant your thoughts of stress with musings of appreciation for the result you wish for.

In the event that you have gained more confidence, this is an ideal opportunity to connect with it. Here is a model:

Rather than stressing over my friends and family going into a terrible climate, I state the following (I consider it a prayer):

"Much thanks to you incredible Jesus for looking out for _________. Much thanks to you for looking out for his/her vehicle and protecting it, street commendable, and liberated from upkeep issues. Much obliged to you for encompassing him/her with just protecting the

faithful and ready drivers. Also, thank you for keeping him/her pro-tected, faithful, and cautious."

Grin when you consider or state it so anyone might hear, express it in the current state; both of these will assist you with feeling it and potentially even begin to trust it.

In the event that you can picture what you are petitioning God for, the representation will upgrade the inclination so you will expand the effect in your vibrational field.

Presently take a breath, gradually in through your nose and out through the mouth. Take the same number as often as you like!

Supplanting frightful thoughts with appreciation will diminish reactionary conduct, removing the steam from the Reactor.

For instance:

In the event that your child loses all sense of direction in the shopping center, the run of the mill parental response that follows the frightful contemplations when discovering them is to shout out, "I told you to never leave my sight." This response adds to the youngster's dread level from being lost in any case. Furthermore, it also instructs them that their mother or father will become distraught when the individual commits an error, which may make them lie to you or not reveal to you about things later on.

Change those frightful musings when they occur:

"Much obliged to you (your decision of Higher Power) for looking out for my child and guarding him. Much thanks to you for helping me discover him soon."

At that point, when you see your kid after this manner of thinking, your solitary response will be appreciation, and that appears as though a superior option for all individuals are included.

3. For the Trouble-Maker, Reactor or Over-Reactor

Disposing of this squatter once and for all will take more consideration and reflection afterward to distinguish and mend the reasons for the triggers; yet up to that point, you can forestall the Reactor from getting out of control by starting cognizant breathing when you perceive his essence.

The Reactor's thoughts or emotions initiate the battle of fight-or-flight reaction simply like it does with the Worrier. The physiological indications of his essence will be the equivalent. With a little consideration, you ought to have the option to differentiate between anxiety, outrage, dissatisfaction, or torment:

In any case, you can beat this anxiety!

I'm certain you've heard the proposal to tally to ten when you're about to blow up, well you can make those ten seconds significantly more gainful in the event that you're breathing intentionally during that time.

Cognizant breathing is as straightforward as it sounds; simply be aware of your relaxing. Focus on the air going in and coming out.

Take in through your nose:

- Feel the air entering your nose
- Your lungs filling and extending
- In your belly rising

- Out through your nose
- Feel your lungs emptying
- Concentrate on your belly falling
- Feel the air exit your nose

Do this for whatever length of time. This gives the adrenaline time to standardize.

Presently you can address the circumstance with a quieter, more increasingly level-headed viewpoint and abstain from harming conduct. One of the difficulties this squatter causes is that it adds to the rest Depriver's issues. By removing, or if nothing else controlling the Reactor, you will diminish reactionary conduct, which will diminish the requirement for the repeating and ruminating that may shield you from nodding off.

Master your mind and prevent the Reactor from carrying worry to you and your relationships with people!

4. For the Sleep Depriver

(They're comprised of the Inner Planner, the Rehasher and the Ruminator, alongside the Inner Critic and the Worrier.)

I was tormented with an exceptionally regular issue: not having the option to kill my mind at sleep time. This powerlessness kept me from nodding off and getting a serene and therapeutic night's rest.

Here's the manner by which I aced my mind and ousted the Sleep Depriver and every one of its cohorts.

I began by concentrating on my breathing, focusing on the rise and fall of my stomach, yet that didn't keep the thoughts out for long (In reality, I started with checking my still mouth position to shield me from holding).

At that point I concocted a substitution system that disposed of uncontrolled reasoning and envisioned the word while taking in and thoroughly considering the word when breathing out. I would (and do) extend the word to coordinate the length of my breath.

At the point when I find myself thinking, I move back to breathing in, then out. With this method, the wheels aren't turning wild again. I'm in charge of my brain and I pick the calm.

From the first occasion when I attempted this strategy I began to yawn after a couple of cycles and I normally snooze within ten minutes.

For extremely troublesome evenings, I include an expansion of consideration by holding my eyes in a looking-into position (Closed, obviously!). Once in a while I attempt to look toward my third eye, however that truly harms my eyes.

In the event that you experience difficulty nodding off and you can't close off your psyche, I unequivocally suggest you attempt this system. I use it consistently. You can begin resting better this evening!

You can utilize this method whenever you need to:

- Fall back to rest in the event that you wake up too early
- Close down your reasoning
- Quiet your emotions
- Basically, center on the current minute

The Bottom Line

Your mind is an apparatus, and like some other instrument, it very well may be utilized for productive purposes or for damaging purposes.

You can permit your brain to be involved by undesirable, bothersome, and ruinous inhabitants, or you can pick alluring occupants like harmony, appreciation, sympathy, love, and satisfaction.

Your brain can turn into your closest companion, your greatest supporter, and somebody you can rely on to be there and energize you. The decision is yours.

Logical Limitations of Our Minds

The mind is a significant tool to assist us with survival in this materialistic, relative world. We are used to the mind weaving unpredictable mazes of perspectives, mind maps, and critical thinking procedures which obviously helps us "adapt" and "endure." From one perspective, the brain's operations are the way into our endurance. Then again, they foil our capacity to live well.

The mind fears that you will essentially close it down like a creation line which is never again required. The brain can't drive you to go well beyond yourself. Neither does it have the instruments to do so. It proposes a wide range of techniques to make you think significantly and more profoundly, understand crossword puzzles, and ceaselessly train yourself "intellectually." It needs you to engage in convoluted conversations where you wind up quarreling, considering, and concentrating on specific technicalities.

I. **Believing is a Wild Monkey**

What occurs in our psyches is unadulterated bedlam. Our thoughts are unrestrained, acting like jumping monkeys and bouncing from one branch then onto the next. "Believing is a wild monkey," said Zen Master Linji. Truth be told, believing is a befuddling mess!

The reason for the presence of your brain is to empower you to utilize it to change your experience and information into knowledge. Your mind places what you have realized is available to you. This permits you to store, re-use and draw upon it at whatever point you like. In any case, the mind has another proclivity. It misuses your encounters to divert you from living right now.

II. **It Drives You Away from the Present Time and Place**

This is a direct result of your psyche's affinity to mull over and harp on about everything conceivable, it incorporates the musings behind your contemplations – rather than its being in the present time and place. It ought to be noticed that the mind has such helpful aptitudes as the capacity to avert hurt by foreseeing and arranging. In any case, it also hauls along a difficult and overwhelming knapsack whose size changes relying upon the person. This "knapsack" is brimming with our encounters of the past and the decisions – apparently fortunate or unfortunate – that we have articulated on them. The brain also contains qualms, misgivings, fears, dreams, and dreams about what is to come.

III. **All I know is That I Know Nothing**

The celebrated explanation credited to the Greek rationalist Socrates, "All I know is that I know nothing," brings up that the sensible mind can't get a handle on the Absoluteness.

The brain can't apply itself to make intelligence bloom exponentially. Rationale comes up short on the capacity and takes us where we have to go. How might we trust it is conceivable to utilize an instrument with innate cut-off points – our brains – to find what is vast and boundless?

IV. **You Mind Resembles a Full Teacup**

There are numerous adaptations of a notable anecdote about a college educator who visited Zen Master Nan-in during the Meiji period in Japan, and was welcome to drink some tea. The Zen Master poured tea until the educator's cup was full, and afterward continued pouring until the tea was everywhere throughout the table and on the floor.

The educator importuned him to stop in light of the fact that the cup was point full. Nan-in answered, "Your brain resembles this teacup. You are so loaded with your own feelings, information and preferences that nothing more can be included. Void your brain with the goal that you can discover some new information."

At the point when the mind stays in stillness and when thinking has at long last halted, development turns out to be profound peacefulness, and you make the way for the heavenly.

Try Not to Let Your Mind Limit, Go Beyond Limiting Thoughts

"The breaking point is not in the sky. The cut-off is the mind." ~Unknown

In spite of the fact that the mind may have some physical limitations, the genuine cut-off is keeping us away from accomplishing our fantasies and are only the limiters we place for ourselves in our brain.

I have often heard the sentence, "Stick to what you know best," and I trust you have heard it as well. As a child, it appeared it was the correct thought, yet as I grew up, I felt the opposite.

I want to utilize various words, "Don't let your brain limit your opportunity of progress." I accept these words and attempt to live as indicated by them.

Venture beyond just dreaming. Figure out how to achieve your dreams! It doesn't make a difference what your present truth is.

Some Testing Questions

- Do you think that it's hard to stare off into space past your present reality?
- Do you permit restricting thoughts to decide your present and future?
- Do you think that it's hard to envision yourself monetarily steady, having a great job, owning a decent house, and getting a charge out of an upbeat life?
- Do you in some cases let yourself know?
- I shouldn't point excessively high, since I'll most certainly come up short.
- For what reason would it be a good idea for me to think about things I will never have?
- Wanting for a higher position is unreasonable, so I better limit myself to what I have now.

- For what reason does such a negative idea run in our psyche?
- For what reason do we permit restricting musings to fill our mind?
- Why not break the obstruction of restricting thoughts?

Each objective we wish to accomplish has at it beginning stage half a possibility of progress and half a possibility of disappointment. In any case, a great many people center on disappointment and increment it into their brain. The sky is the limit from there.

There is no motivation to help the propensity for negative reasoning. This propensity rehashes itself frequently, since we fear disappointment and permit restricting musings to coordinate our life.

We would prefer not to baffle ourselves and others. We dread dismissal, and we don't need individuals to reprimand and disparagement us if we fall flat. These feelings of trepidation keep us from attempting new things.

Fears Are Limiting Thoughts

Most feelings of trepidation are simply constraining musings that run in our mind and make sickening mental situations about what may occur when we fall flat and what individuals may think about our disappointment.

The Positive Phase of Fear

Fear can't be entirely negative. It has a positive and valuable side, securing and guarding us. It is a major admonition sign on our street in life that advises us not to face challenges that may imperil our security. Fear cautions us not to sink our reserve funds in a fishy business, it cautions us not to walk alone in a dim pathway, and it alerts us not to dive into a shallow lake.

Fear gets us far from risky circumstances that may put our life in danger. In any case, a lot of dread prompts a restricted reasoning and constrained life, and can transform into a significant obstruction to progress.

How might you feel the fear, yet set out and follow your objectives:

- What do you have to do in the event that you need an achievement?
- What can build your odds of making progress?
- Recognize your feelings of dread, and become mindful of your restricting musings
- Quit building shocking mental situations about what may occur if you fall flat
- Make room in your mind for a positive and hopeful mentality
- Plan for an impressive future. Try not to restrain your creative mind to your present life
- Picture in your mind how effective you are in your preferred field

Our life's conditions may define mental and passionate limits, however, we can cross them by changing our thoughts and demeanor, and by preparing to stun the world regardless of what our present conditions are.

You can keep on restricting yourself and your life by tolerating your limits and adhering to your present reality.

You can also accept how you can improve your life, and venture past your current conditions and limits.

Let me explain this thought with a model:

Envision yourself viewing a specific film throughout the day for quite a while. In time, the film would get exhausting and uninteresting, yet you keep watching it, in light of the fact that the demonstration of viewing a similar film has become a propensity. You became accustomed to this, and the thought that you have the alternative to watch an alternate film doesn't occur.

This propensity for adhering to the old and recognizable, dismissing new thoughts and new exercises, and accepting that you are unequipped for managing new encounters restrains your soul, keeps you down, and keeps you from making yourself more aware.

This negative propensity makes you keep carrying on with a similar sort of life and thinking similar thoughts inside a similar amount of conceivable outcomes.

For instance:

- You convey in your mind the picture of your present place of employment, not the picture of a superior activity
- Your thoughts rotate around your current money related condition, and not on getting rich
- You center around your present conditions, and not on a more extravagant and joyful way of life

This sort of reasoning sustains similar conditions. You continue pulling in comparative occasions, circumstances and conditions into your life, and don't make place for anything new or better.

You can quit thinking about constraining your thoughts, or show your mind to think greater and more pleasant musings.

Our Limitations and How to Go Beyond Them

For what reason do we stall, quit, worry ourselves, beat ourselves up, and grow unfortunate propensities? For what reason do we become the cause of all our own problems rather than our own closest companion?

Our psyches are fascinating things. They're so incredible, but such huge numbers of individuals don't have the foggiest idea how to utilize them to their advantage.

We needn't bother with an enchantment pill like in the film, Limitless, to vanquish our psyches. We needn't bother with military preparing us to become priests and build up the controls that will enable us to succeed.

We simply need to comprehend why we think the manner in which we do and discover approaches to make ourselves think the manner in which we need to think. At the end of the day, we should think of what serves us, rather than a way that keeps us down.

Napoleon Hill, author of "Think and Grow Rich," stated, "Our lone restrictions are the ones we set up in our own minds." Throughout the years, I've discovered that he is correct. On the off chance that we vanquish our psyches, we can accomplish anything.

The Meaning of Napoleon Hill's Quote

Our mind is amazingly incredible, however, that doesn't mean it generally works to support us. What we feed it figures out what we receive in return.

It's much the same as placing the best possible fuel into a vehicle, we need to fuel our minds with the correct thoughts. We must know about what we are considering rather than simply tolerating our present convictions.

Convictions can be changed. We don't need to acknowledge them for what they are at present, but the same number of individuals often do. A considerable lot of us have been affected by individuals with negative perspectives of the world.

A significant number of us haven't been raised to think like the fruitful individuals do. Yet, the insignificant conviction is a reason and negative idea that doesn't serve you. It's an inappropriate sort of fuel for your brain.

Napoleon Hill shows us in his books that you should make your musings serve you, not moderate you down. We possibly have limit that we permit in our psyches.

We just dawdle and we don't know about what we're doing or have a conviction that lingering is alright. We just have antagonistic convictions since we permit other fruitless individuals to impact us.

Our thoughts are intended to serve you in a manner that makes bliss and causes you accomplish whatever objectives you have.

If you would begin monitoring your thoughts, convictions, and the propensities your mind has set up, you could find a way to transform them after some time to assist you with turning out who you really want to be.

Activity Steps

Here are a couple of steps you can take to apply the exercise instructed by Napoleon Hill:

1. In the first place, know about your reasoning. Take a look at your mind like it is as a third individual, watching to perceive what it will do in various circumstances.

2. Record your top beliefs and propensities genuinely for the duration of the day. Do this for as long as seven days. Do something very similar with your propensities. To make your mind work for you, you should know about where it presently is.

3. Ask yourself what you need throughout everyday life. Do you need bliss? Would you like to be a mogul entrepreneur? Would you like to be sound with a fit body? Record these objectives.

4. Presently, experience your convictions just as habits and ask yourself whether they help or keep you away from accomplishing your objectives.

5. Presently you ought to have a thought of what requirements need to change. Perhaps you need to be sound, yet you have a propensity for eating sweets after each feast. Perhaps you need to be progressively beneficial, yet you continue thinking it's alright to constantly put off significant assignments.

6. Work on changing these propensities, musings, and convictions that keep you down. Supplant sugar with organic products. Begin

doing significant assignments first so you don't put them off. Begin perusing a section every day about how to manufacture a fruitful business. Quit filling your brain with negative news. Abstain from spending time with individuals who have no goals throughout their everyday life.

7. Continue doing these mind assessments week by week, month to month, or regularly, so you can ensure you're on target or assist yourself with making a couple of new changes.

Your accomplishment in completing any objective descends to your mind and how much control you have over it. Continuously act mindful of your contemplations and what your propensities are to decide whether they server you.

Step by **S**tep **I**nstructions to go **B**eyond Limiting Thoughts

Here are a couple of rules for discharging your negative musings and embracing positive ones:

1. The first and most significant advance to do is to be mindful of the constraining thoughts that run in your psyche.

2. Next, supplant the constraining and negative thoughts with positive musings, which are something contrary to restricting contemplations.

How would you do that? Each time a negative idea enters your psyche, promptly supplant it with a positive one.

Regardless of what your present truth is, and regardless of what your past experience is, envision achievement, satisfaction, and great connections, rather than foreseeing disappointment, dismissal, and dissatisfaction.

3. If you come up short, as it every so often may occur, consider this disappointment a stage on the stepping stool to progress, and next time increment your endeavors.

4. Rehash certifications about the objectives and things you wish to accomplish.

5. Increment your motivation, elevate your spirits, and addition new points of view on life, by perusing moving anecdotes about individuals who made progress.

6. You may think in a constrained manner, putting a psychological hindrance around you, and you may break the obstruction and think greater and better musings. It's all in the brain, a restricted and boundless life. Everything relies upon how you think.

Bit by bit, as you continue being industrious with your new demeanor, your brain will quit thinking about constraining contemplations and begin embracing another, greater and more useful perspective. At that point, new chances and new ways to progress will introduce themselves to you, which you will be capable to notice, grasp, and follow.

With a little day by day exertion on your part, you will figure out how to quit constraining thoughts and defeat them.

Believe in yourself. You will gain the power to overcome.

Steps to Become Master of Your Own Mind

Huge numbers of individuals invest an over the top measure of time and vitality — also cash — in dealing with our bodies, and attempting to keep ourselves looking and feeling our best. Be that as it may, with regards to the brain, less consideration is paid. Dealing with the brain can come as a bit of hindsight, and frequently we think about the mind as something outside of our own control.

"Our life is the making of our psyche," as indicated by Buddhist sacred writing. The Buddhist way of thinking built up a whole study of preparing the raucous mind to assist anybody with beating its steady variances to accomplish stillness, and in the end, edification.

In any case, regardless of whether it's not illumination is what you're subsequent to, building up a decent connection with your mind is basic to building an actual existence that is fruitful on your own terms. Here are eight propensities for brain development for less stress, greater inventiveness, not so much interruption but rather more happiness throughout everyday life.

I. Seek after importance over joy

Not all satisfaction is made equivalent, and in your own quest for euphoria and joy, remember that the sort of bliss you're after can have a significant effect. An ongoing UCLA study found that eudemonic bliss — which was connected to having a bigger reason or feeling of significance throughout everyday life — was connected with sound strength movement, though decadent, or joy chasing, but satisfaction was definitely not found. The individuals who were cheerful on the grounds that they had a feeling of direction in life had lower provocative strength, articulation, and higher antiviral and neutralizer strength articulation than others.

"Eudaimonia satisfaction is something you develop over a lifetime," Shimon Edelman, Cognitive therapist and creator of "The Happiness of Pursuit," told The Huffington Post. "It could be said, it's an incredible relief for more established individuals — it's pleasant to realize that on that segment, individuals can get increasingly gladder as they age on the off chance that they had great existences."

ii. Peruse, Read, and Read

Basically, perusing a book can bring down feelings of anxiety, assist you with dozing better, keep your mind sharp, and furthermore fight off Alzheimer's.

In any case, before you go to your Kindle, observe: reading on screens may deplete mental assets and make it harder to recollect what we've perused after we're done, when contrasted with perusing on paper, as per Scientific American.

"Regardless of whether they understand it or not, individuals frequently approach PCs and tablets with a perspective less helpful for learning than the one they bring to paper," as indicated by the article.

iii. Leave it Alone

Sweating the little stuff is one of the most dangerous things you can do to your mind. Not exclusively would it be able to assume control over your thoughts, yet harping on about what is outside your ability of control has been demonstrated to be a contributing variable in the advancement of sadness.

Have you realized that incomplete task that's been bothering you? Attempt by simply releasing it. As per Arianna Huffington, an extraordinary method to finish an undertaking is by dropping it. Huffington as of late clarified at a Women in Business occasion in Toronto:

"One of my preferred truisms is '100 percent is a breeze, 99 percent is a bitch'... That doesn't mean overlooking my different needs, yet it implies when I'm in it, I'm truly in it. Furthermore, that implies regularly disapproving of beneficial things, to things that you should do, yet impede rest, or hinder being with your kids, or whatever it is that is likewise imperative to you. Simply have a discussion with yourself and state these undertakings are done, over, and afterward you have vitality for the things you're truly going to subscribe to."

iv. Utilize Your Memory Muscle

On account of innovation, we're taking in more information than any other time in recent memory, but at the same time we're losing our capacity to hold that information. An ongoing survey found that twenty to thirty-year-olds are significantly more neglectful than seniors, due to their dependence on innovation.

Keeping your memory sharp requires some time and consideration, however, your mind will thank you for it. Certain psychological activities can fundamentally support your forces of memory, and ensure that you clutch onto those things you never need to overlook.

v. Unplug and Revive

Steady advanced interruptions can negatively affect the over dependence on innovation and has been connected with expanded feelings of anxiety, decreased concentration and efficiency, hindered imagination, and poor rest strength. Furthermore, Internet enslavement is progressively being perceived as an undeniable mental issue.

A large number of people never enjoy a reprieve from our gadgets, when we should be unwinding (about 60 percent of Americans remain connected to work while they're in the midst of a get-away). In any case, portioning yourself without tech time could make you progressively centered, less pushed, and more joyful.

"[An advanced detox] is practically similar to a reboot for your mind and your spirit," Cisco official Padmasree Warrior told the New York Times. "It makes me so a lot more settled when I'm reacting to messages later."

vi. Allow Your Mind to Meander

Boosting innovativeness by staring off into space can really make you more astute.

As indicated by NYU clinician Scott Kaufman's hypothesis of individual knowledge, mind-meandering is a versatile attribute that causes us to accomplish significant objectives, and it encourages us to get to unconstrained types of perception like understanding, instinct and the activating of recollections and put away information.

Kaufman as of late wrote in Scientific American that mind-meandering can offer noteworthy individual prizes:

"These prizes incorporate mindfulness, imaginative hatching, act of spontaneity and assessment, memory union, self-portraying arranging, objective driven idea, future arranging, recovery of profoundly close to home recollections, intelligent thought of the significance of occasions and encounters, recreating the viewpoint of someone else, assessing the ramifications of self as well as other people's passionate responses, moral thinking, and intelligent sympathy... From this individual point of view, it is a lot more obvious why individuals are attracted to mind meandering and ready to contribute almost 50 percent of their waking hours occupied with it."

vii Linger on the Positive

Need to wire your mind for satisfaction? You can begin by appreciating those small snapshots of euphoria in your day, regardless of whether it's the smell of new espresso or a grin from a friend or family member. Waiting on these positives can assist with defeating the mind's "pessimism predisposition," which makes us store negative recollections in our brains rather than positive recollections.

"[Lingering on the positive] improves the encoding of passing mental states into enduring neural characteristics," "Designing Happiness" creator Rick Hanson as of late told the Huffington Post. "That is the key here: we're attempting to get the great stuff into us. Furthermore, that implies transforming our passing positive encounters into enduring enthusiastic recollections."

viii. Manufacture Every Day Customs

Propensity is one of the best approaches to roll out any positive improvement in your life. By creating propensities, great practices that may have once required an accomplishment of determination to place enthusiastically get programmed, which is the reason they can also be so hard to break.

"For the things that you choose matter ... the best way to guarantee that things aren't dire yet are significant happen is to assemble customs," The Energy Project CEO Tony Schwartz told the Huffington Post. "Manufacture profoundly explicit practices that you do at exact occasions again and again until you don't need to utilize vitality to get yourself to do it any longer — until it becomes as programmed as brushing your teeth around evening time."

CHAPTER 3

GROWTH MINDSET: HOW TO MASTER YOUR MIND AND CREATE THE LIFE YOU WANT

Growth Mindset

Your brain holds the ability to assist you to prevail any everyday issue, except without an outlook concentrated on development.

Building up a development mentality has become a well-known point since individuals have understood its gigantic effect on progress potential.

Yet, beginning it can be confounding. There's been a surge of information from researchers, otherworldly pioneers, business symbols, and VIPs who all have their own interpretation of the subject.

It very well may be difficult to tell where to begin and who to tune in to.

We will make it simpler for you to begin building up a development outlook so you can start to receive the astonishing rewards of riches, health, and bliss.

What Is A Growth Mindset?

In any case, I don't get its meaning to have a development mentality?

On one level, it's tied in with needing to make a superior life and concentrating on self-improvement so you can accomplish it. That incorporates inspecting and changing your convictions and ongoing contemplations.

Going somewhat more profound, there's one key conviction that you should have, or receive, to make any further development conceivable. The conviction you are fit for developing!

In the event that you think something is conceivable, you will find (or even make) a confirmation that it is. What's more, the inverse is additionally valid.

Since your brain has such a major effect with an amazing result in understanding, you're consistently making inevitable outcomes.

Your outcomes come down to which predictions you have faith in and reinforce.

In the event that you trust you can change, learn, and develop, you'll likely discover you're correct. This opens up boundless opportunities for you.

What's more, in the event that you accept you're left with whatever abilities or characteristics you were brought into the world with, at that point you have confidence in a constrained reality.

Along these lines, in the event that you need to have the option to change and develop, the main conviction you have to develop is that you can!

This is actually what a development mentality is tied in with — trusting you can build up the abilities and attributes you have to accomplish your objectives.

The Science of Growth Mindset

This thought may sound basic on a superficial level. In any case, it's been intricate enough to keep researchers concentrating on every one of its subtleties and applications for a long time. Sespite everything, they're making new disclosures.

Prestigious Stanford University specialist Carol Dweck instituted the expressions "development outlook" and "fixed attitude" subsequent to understanding a great many subjects' reactions to challenge and disappointment.

A development attitude expects that accomplishments and disappointments come generally from exertion and advancement, or a deficiency in that department.

A fixed attitude expects that attributes are innate and essentially unchangeable, constraining what we can realize, do, and accomplish.

Studies show that building up a development outlook prompts more prominent strength and more significant levels of accomplishment.

Step by Step Instructions to Know If You Need Mindset Work

The human psyche, left undeveloped, tends to become stagnated in familiar areas, which in turn shields us from accomplishing our objectives.

It's not our flaw — it's simply human instinct.

The uplifting news is you can take mindfulness of business. Through preparing, practice, and training, you can redesign your attitude.

The key is to reveal any routine thoughts and convictions that aren't serving you and change them into better ones.

How about we take a look at some indications that you may profit from by using attitude work.

- ☐ Do you ever get too focused or overpowered?
- ☐ Do you feel your life is out of equalization or missing something?
- ☐ Do you regularly feel depleted, stuck, overpowered, or on a passionate roller-coaster?
- ☐ Do you put off doing things that would push your life ahead?
- ☐ Do you experience difficulty finishing your thoughts and dreams? Do you settle on decisions dependent on dread of passing up a great opportunity or dread of offending someone?
- ☐ Is it accurate to say that you are awkward saying no?
- ☐ Is it accurate to say that you fear being told no?
- ☐ Do you experience any difficulties with decision-making?

In the event that you've addressed yes to any or the entirety of the above mentioned, attitude work could make a number of positive effects happen.

Why Avoiding Mindset Work Is a Mistake

Self-awareness has developed into an enormous industry. Yet, numerous individuals — despite everything —don't prefer to concede that they probably won't be great or have everything in perfect order.

Tragically, numerous individuals avoid attitude work, regardless of the demonstrated advantages in light of a social disgrace about apparent mental or enthusiastic shortcoming.

In any case, what's the expense of not accomplishing mindset work?

Celebrated achievement educator Jim Rohn stated, "In the event that you continue doing what you've constantly done, you'll continue getting what you've generally got."

What's the after effect of proceeding to think, feel, and have confidence in your equivalent ongoing manners?

You'll keep settling on similar choices, take similar sorts of activities, and get similar outcomes.

You may even make your psychological examples more grounded through redundancy. Those examples can hard-wire themselves into your mind.

Neuropsychologist Donald Hebb instructed that "neurons that fire together wire together."

This implies constant musings fortify themselves.

They fabricate physical associations in the brain each time we think them. It gets simpler to continue thinking in similar manners.

Negative convictions and responses can get more grounded sometime after except if you rehearse and impart various examples. This is the pith of attitude work.

The Benefits of Developing a Growth Mindset

1. So what would you be able to expect in the event that you deal with building up your mentality?

2. At the beginning, you may feel good, less on edge or tense, increasingly serene and content. Little aggravations don't trouble you as much as they used to, or if nothing else not as long.

3. Your contemplations may turn out to be all the clearer, or you may turn out to be progressively centered on where you need to end your life and organize the things that issue to you.

4. You may start caring more for your health, prompting more vitality and essentialness.

Furthermore, this could make you more appealing to your present accomplice or potential ones in case you're single.

Anything you desire and mindfulness about, your outlook is the spot to moving in the direction of it.

Envision you needed to send a rocket to the moon.

You'd need all engines pointing their vitality the correct way, wouldn't you?

That is how a development attitude accomplishes from your vitality. It impels you toward your objectives.

How a Growth Mindset Leads to Success

Things being what they are, how precisely does your attitude have such a monstrous impact on your life?

In the first place, as Harv has frequently educated at his workshops, your mind goes about as a channel for your encounters.

It resembles wearing tinted glasses where the shade of the focal point decides what everything looks like.

Be that as it may, the focal point of your brain includes something considerably more remarkable than shading. It includes meaning.

Lisa Quay is Executive Director of the Mindset Scholars Network. She clarified that exploration shows how individuals "make importance of circumstances, others, and themselves shapes how they react."

"The impact is most grounded in the midst of challenge and vulnerability," she said. What's more, the impact of your brain doesn't stop with how it influences your own decisions and conduct.

She proceeded to express that your conduct influences how your general surroundings react to you, molding into an amazing course.

With the correct outlook, you could begin to settle on better choices that help you accomplish what you need.

You may make a superior showing of your work and make more associations, prompting an advancement or a raise. Or then again begin to take greater steps with your side hustle. You could land new customers and better-paying gigs.

Every improvement in your outlook swells out through your decisions and your activities.

This progression impacts the individuals and situations around you. Those impacts point that back at you, upgrading your own life.

Top Resources and Tools for Mindset Training

Mentality improvement implies finding out about your routine musings and instilled convictions. And afterward, changing the ones that aren't helping you.

You could learn systems to revamp your idea designs, for example, Neuro-Linguistic Programming and mental Freedom Technique.

You could attempt mantra reflection to center your brain. Journaling may assist you with seeing any negative contemplations or convictions you convey. Furthermore, enabling insistences could help train new idea designs.

What's more, remember to incorporate your body, which is hard-wired to your brain.

Indeed, even things as basic as changing your stance, grinning, or getting your blood siphoning can improve your psychological and enthusiastic state.

Every one of these apparatuses can assist you with developing a mentality of progress and development.

However, you must have the order and aptitudes to utilize them successfully, so it tends to be difficult to change them all alone.

You aren't the only one! We as a whole have predispositions and vulnerable sides, particularly about the manners on what we think and what we accept.

We don't have the foggiest idea, but we can't generally perceive the suspicions we've made about ourselves and the world.

So, it very well may be a distinct advantage to work with a mentor or coach who sees how the mind functions and how to change its propensities.

Truth be told, a report from Mindset Scholars Network expressed that " ... sheer exertion can't. The correct procedures and guidance from others are similarly significant for reinforcing the mind."

A decent mentor could bolster you with objective setting, control, and core interest.

They could also help with certainty, self-esteem, making better propensities, venturing out of your usual range of familiarity, and more.

Working with a mentor doesn't mean there's a major issue with you.

The top entertainers in any field, from sports to business, all have mentors or tutors.

This encourages them to continue improving the issue that affect them the most.

The Most Effective Method to Choose a Mindset Coach

Be cautious while picking a mentor. Numerous individuals get into instructing with honest goals, however, absent a lot of progress added to their repertoire.

A decent mentor will have accomplished the sorts of things you need to accomplish and accomplished the work by themselves.

Also, they'll have a reputation of helping other people get the sort of results you're searching for.

Private coaching can be costly, yet we live in the age of the web. We can access and offer information at practically no expense.

To master your work, you must work to master your mind.

The Inner Game of Tennis must be the most unusual book on self-improvement I've had at any point. Apparently, it's not composed as a manual for improving your tennis match-up, it's actually a manual on mental authority and high-accomplishment.

The center contention of the book is at the most significant levels of execution — it's not specialized — are explicit aptitudes that figure out who succeeds and who doesn't. Everybody who gets to the highest point of their field has just aced a large portion of these specialized aptitudes.

Rather, the most elite can accomplish and support top execution and greatness since they've figured out how to ace what the creator calls "The Inner Game." Through the taught advancement of our psychological propensities, we permit our fullest potential and capacity to communicate without impedance or limitation. Along these lines, to ace your work in any region, you should learn first to ace your own psyche.

What follows is an assortment of citations from the book followed by my own concise contemplations and reflections on them.

On Mastery

Neither dominance nor fulfillment can be found in the playing of any game without concentrating on the moderately disregarded abilities of the internal game. This is the game that happens in the brain of the player, and it is played against such snags as breaches in focus, apprehension, self-uncertainty and self-judgment. To put it plainly, it is played to defeat all propensities of the mind which restrains greatness in execution.

The vast majority of us don't have the foggiest idea about the internal game being played, and it's significantly less that we're losing.

Time to suit up.

On Potential

At the point when we plant a rose seed in the earth, we notice that it is little, however, we don't censure it as "rootless and stemless." We treat it as a seed, giving it the water and sustenance expected of a seed. At the point when it first shoots up out of the earth, we don't censure it as youthful and immature; nor do we reprimand the buds for not being open when they show up. We remain in wonder at the procedure occurring and give the plant the consideration it needs at each phase of its improvement. The rose is a rose from the time it is a seed to the time it passes on. Inside it, consistently, it contains its entire potential. It is by all accounts continually changing during the time spent at each state, at every minute.

Envision how your life may be unique in the event that you truly accepted this: I have inside me, consistently, my entire potential.

On Letting Go

Relinquishing decisions doesn't mean disregarding mistakes. It just means considering occasions to be what they are and don't add to them.

I presume a main explanation is that numerous individuals make some hard memories with ideas like acknowledgment, care, and non-judgment. These terms suggest a sort of lack of involvement and shortcoming, but in any case, nothing could be further from reality.

Deciding to see reality for what it is without anticipating our own thoughts onto it is for all intents and purposes a superpower.

On Effort

The key to dominating any match lies in not making a decent attempt.

Applying heaps of conscious practice and exertion when you are learning an expertise will produce results. In any case, with regards to utilizing the ability in a true circumstance, exertion will meddle with what you've just realized and know.

On Self-Judgment

It is intriguing to perceive how the critical brain expands itself. It might start by whining, "What a lousy serve," at that point it stretches out to "I'm serving seriously today." After a couple of increasingly "awful" serves, the judgment may turn out to reach out to "I have a horrendous serve." The, "I'm a lousy tennis player," changes to, "I'm nothing more than a bad memory." First the brain makes a decision about the occasion, at that point bunches occasions, at that point relates to the joined occasion until it passes judgment on itself.

This is the reason it's fundamental to figure out how to rapidly get and divert negative self-talk. On the off chance that it goes unchecked, this endless loop of self-judgment and disgrace it creates rapidly turns out to be gigantic to the point that it's difficult to escape from.

As an old educator of mine used to state: Falling off the wagon isn't the issue; it's the floundering around in the mud that murders you.

Develop consciousness of your own self-talk so you can halt it from the beginning.

On Bad Habits

It is hard to get out from under a propensity when there is no suffi-cient substitution for it.

A result of this is shockingly simple to get out from under negative behavior patterns and to set up positive ones when you have an im-portant, fulfilling, obviously characterized vision for an elective pro-pensity that meets indistinguishable requirements from the former one of a more advantageous, progressively gainful way.

On Labels

Critical marks for the most part lead to enthusiastic responses and afterward to snugness, making a decent attempt, self-judgment, and so forth. This procedure can be eased back by utilizing spellbinding, however, non-judgmental words portray the occasions you see.

For execution to move toward potential, escape your own particular manner and permit your hard-won ability to radiate through.

Obviously, this is more difficult than one might expect. At the point when we're in the psychological propensity for critical self-talk, it can feel progressively like something that transpires as opposed to some-thing we have command over.

Instead of attempting to stop or take out this critical self-talk, swarm it out with straightforward perception and depiction.

On Positive Thinking

It is difficult to pass judgment on one occasion as positive without considering the other to be as not positive or as negative.

Positive reasoning is similar to critical reasoning. Keeping in mind that it might quickly feel great since it's sure, we effectively slip starting with one type of judgment onto the next.

Why not judge all together and basically notice things as they seem to be?

On Identity

In the event that a mother relates to each fall of her child and invests heavily on each achievement, her mental self-view will be as temperamental as her youngster's parity.

Be cautious where you decide to contribute your personality and feeling of self.

Anything outside of your immediate control is commonly a poor vehicle for personality investment — other individuals, explicit emotions, cash, and distinction.

Better personality speculation incorporates difficult work, thoughtfulness, interest, learning, liberality, and the such.

On Inner Peace

The most ideal approach to calm the brain can't be telling it to quiet down, or by contending with it, or censuring it for scrutinizing you. Battling the mind doesn't work. What works best is figuring out how to center it.

You've presumably heard the expression: what we oppose perseveres.

The inquiry is: okay, I'll quit opposing ... presently what?

It's insufficient to just move our consideration away from an ineffective line of reasoning like contending with our own thoughts. We should get talented in the specialty of diverting our thoughtfulness regarding something progressively significant and beneficial. This has two sections:

Make them bid elective objects of consideration nearby. Develop objects of consideration that lead to harmony instead of stress. Side interests are acceptable.

Practice the "move" of moving your consideration starting with one item then onto the next. Develop a consideration preparing routine.

On Competition

The need to substantiate yourself depends on frailty and self-question. Just to the degree that one is uncertain about who and what he is, does this mean he has to substantiate himself?

Here's an oddity of superior brain research: the less your personality is on the line while playing out, the better you will perform in light of the fact that the risk of harming our character consistently meddles with our execution.

Leave your self-uninvolved.

On Concentration

The best passes in fixation come when we permit our psyches to extend what is going to occur or harp on about what has just occurred.

The limit with respect to mental time travel is apparently our species' most significant blessing and mental favorable position. Since we can recollect the past and envision what's to come, we're equipped for gigantic accomplishments. It also frees us up from stress, rumination, and interruption.

For your mental health and your efficiency, work on holding your consideration in the present time and place.

On Control

Strength develops as you figure out how to acknowledge what you can't control and assume responsibility for what you can.

The general purpose of training and readiness is that our psyches and bodies figure out how to accomplish our ideal objectives and results. For high-achievers, poor readiness and absence of exertion an issue every once in a while. We end up damaging ourselves by making a decent attempt and meddling with what we've just prepared ourselves to achieve.

This misapplication of exertion is an issue of control. To arrive at the most noteworthy echelons of accomplishment, we should be happy to discharge control and confide in ourselves.

On Focus

Since the mind appears to have its very own will, how might one figure out how to keep it present? By training. There is no other way. Each time your brain begins to release away, bring it tenderly back.

At whatever point I talk about the significance of preparing your regard for one article and to tenderly return it to that object when you've gotten diverted, I constantly get the accompanying reaction: "Yeah, no doubt, sounds incredible. Be that as it may, how would I really do it?"

Individuals need a mystery tip, stunt, or hack to improve their attentional capacities and core interest, which resembles saying: "Yeah, however, how would I really jump on the treadmill and begin running?"

On Keeping Your Head

The most essential instrument for individuals in current occasions is the capacity to try and avoid panicking amid fast and disrupting changes. Internal soundness is accomplished not by covering one's head in the sand at seeing peril, however, by questioning the capacity to see the genuine idea of what's going on and to react fittingly.

Perception is the initial phase in the Scientific Method for an explanation: estimating, breaking down, and most different types of believing will be misinformed without a little information first.

On Winning

Wining is defeating obstructions to arrive at an objective, yet the incentive in winning is just as incredible as the estimation of the objective that came.

Objectives without technique are useless, as are procedures without the correct objectives.

Endeavor to be both a strategist and a general, professional and CEO, analyst and logician.

On Excellence

I accept our capacity to flourish and prevail in any domain is characterized by our ability to frame connections.

And keeping in mind that we can accomplish a lot from building associations with things in the outer world — people, places, objects, information, skills — the advancement of authority and the accomplishment of greatness necessitates that we develop a relationship with ourselves, with our own personalities.

CHAPTER 4
UNDERSTANDING WORRY

The Concept of Worry

We should begin at the absolute starting point. What is worry at any rate? It is difficult to attempt to manage something that you don't see, so the initial step is to perceive stress, what it incorporates, and what it implies for you.

If you like, you can pause for a minute to think about your own definition.

Tip: You may think that it's accommodating to have a diary close by to make notes, write down bits of knowledge and record changes in sentiments as you come across them. In the event that you have one within reach, pause for a minute to draw up a couple of sentences that catch the embodiment of stress for you.

How Is Worry Defined?

For the reasons for this course, we'll talk about stress in general terms. We'll utilize "anxiety" and "stress" conversely, however, we'll group stress as:

Any musings, sentiments, pictures, thoughts, and fears, that are largely negative in their temperament and which occur in light of either genuine or envisioned future issues.

How does this contrast with your definition?

Obviously, the wide definition above envelops a considerable amount! This could incorporate worry about an up and coming activity, stress over funds, or upsetting thoughts around your youngsters' future. If you rapidly envision something right now that is irritating you, you'll most likely find that it very well may be named stress that utilizes this definition.

Recognize Your Worries

Presently, as you envision this present stress, inquire whether it's an idea, feeling, picture and so on. If it's negative in nature and if it's genuine or envisioned. This is much harder to do than it appears.

In the case if something is extremely liable to occur or not will not be obvious. For instance, envision one day you locate another and exceptionally weird looking mole on your back, which looks quite hazardous. Recollecting what number of individuals is in your removed family who have had skin malignant growth, you begin to stress — would you be able to have skin disease as well?

Sensible Versus Fanciful Worries

In the accompanying articles, we'll take a look at why your response to an occasion like this is totally one of a kind to you, yet it's under your influence. We've sorted out an expansive diagram of what stress is, yet with regards to the "genuine" versus "fanciful" part, things get precarious. We should look at the following area to perceive how we can differentiate between stresses that are genuine and those that are simply non-existent.

Stresses are situated later on and are fears about what might occur. In any case, not all the things we stress over have a similar possibility of occurring. In addition, regardless of whether there is a solid possibility of something occurring, our agonizing over it frequently doesn't effectively change the reality.

How Likely Is It?

Take a look at the accompanying stressing musings, and choose whether the dread is genuine or fanciful. At the end of the day, how likely the dread is of working out as expected.

- You get an uncommon type of malignant growth from eating some terminated nourishment in your cooler and will kick the bucket inside a month
- You get an uncommon type of disease
- The individual who is late and hasn't messaged you back has been in a terrible fender bender
- You won't have enough cash to put something aside for retirement
- People are talking badly of you despite your good faith
- Your friend is cheating or will inevitably

In the event that you wavered with a portion of these, it's reasonable. Normally, it is increasingly hard to choose if something is genuine or non-existent, whenever you're now agonizing over it or not.

Do You Have Any Control?

A decent method to begin directing and dealing with your stress, be that as it may, can't ask how likely a thing is to occur — all things considered, all of the above could hypothetically, theoretically, occur, rather than asking yourself how much control you have over the circumstance. To a limited extent, we'll look in more detail at methods to do this, yet for the time being, return to the above thoughts and check whether you will change your answers when you ask, "What amount of control do I have about whether or not this occurs?"

Versatile and Maladaptive Worry

How about we ask ourselves again about how much stress is an excessive amount of stress!

Individuals will consider stress as a fixed amount; an unavoidable truth similar to UV radiation or covering charges. In any case, consider what one individual stress is totally unremarkable to another, and a third individual may even make it very decisive.

Same Situation, Different Interpretation

Returning to our skin malignancy model — you may begin to stress horribly, make a medical check-up and stress for quite a long time as you make yourself more on edge perusing terrifying articles on the web. Or, on the other hand, you may make the arrangement and afterward quickly forget about it. It's presumably nothing, isn't that so?

Stress can't be an outside improvement, but instead, a transaction between any life form and its condition. Regardless of whether an improvement gets characterized as upsetting especially relies upon whether that living being has the assets to adequately manage that upgrade. Along these lines, it would be exact to state, "I locate this peculiar mole stressing" than "this odd mole is stressing."

Stressing Has Many Faces

Ordinarily, counsel around stress from the executive's centers advises individuals to quiet down, unwind, possibly hear some out-whale music and contemplate. Nonetheless, I'm certain you can consider somebody in your life who would prefer to pass on than do any of this, and would in actuality locate the entire experience to be unimaginably upsetting! Since everyone has their own assets, adapting aptitudes and methods for deciphering the world, when we state "stress" we only mean a certain something.

Is Your Personal Worry Too Much?

Responding to the inquiry (how much stress is an excessive amount of stress?) turns into something simple. A decent measuring stick to utilize is this: is stress meddling with your capacity to develop, associate with others, fulfill work and family commitments, and for the most part, do what you have to do in your life? Provided that this is true, at that point this can be considered "to an extreme" stress, or maladaptive stress. Then again, your stress is causing you to feel persuaded, motivated and prepared to act, at that point it's almost certain it's versatile stress regardless of what that stress happens to be.

Applied to the Real World

In reality, this implies there is stipend for our individual contrasts. An enormous cut-off time in 12 hours could make a flourishing Wall Street dealer focus on and acknowledge the demand, though the equivalent may make a restless new mother need to pull out her hair.

How Worrying Affects the Body

It is safe to say that you are an unnecessary worrier? Maybe you unwittingly feel that you "stress enough," and can keep awful things from occurring. However, the truth of the matter is stressing can influence the body in manners that may astonish you. When stressing gets over the top, it can prompt sentiments of high tension and even reason you to become genuinely sick.

What Happens with Excessive Worrying?

Stressing is feeling uncomfortable or being excessively worried about a circumstance or issue. With unreasonable stressing, your brain and body go into overdrive as you continually center on "what may occur."

Amid the exorbitant stressing, you may endure with high anxiety — even frenzy — during waking hours. Numerous constant worriers recount feeling an emotion of looming fate or ridiculous apprehensions that alone increments their stresses. Ultra-delicate to their condition and to the analysis of others, exorbitant worriers may see anything and anybody as a potential danger.

Interminable stressing can influence your day by day life so much that it might meddle with your craving, way of life propensities, connections, rest, and occupation execution. Numerous individuals who stress unreasonably are so anxiety ridden that they look for help in hurtful ways of life propensities, for example, indulging, cigarette smoking, or utilizing liquor and medications.

What Is Anxiety?

Anxiety is an ordinary response to stretch. Continuous anxiety, however, might be the after-effect of a confusion, for example, summed up anxiety disorder, panic disorder, or social anxiety. Anxiety issues are typical in the U.S., influencing about 40 million adults. Anxiety shows itself in different manners and doesn't segregate by age, sexual orientation, or race.

Distressing occasions, for example, of a test or a prospective employee meet-up can cause anybody to feel somewhat on edge. Also, in some cases, a little stress or anxiety is useful. It can assist you with preparing for an up and coming circumstance. For example, in case you're planning for a prospective employee meeting, a little stress or tension may push you to discover progressively about the position. At that point you can introduce yourself all the more experienced to the potential business. Stressing over a test may assist you with concentrating more and be progressively arranged on test day.

In any case, over the top worriers respond rapidly and strongly to these distressing circumstances or triggers. In any event, this can cause ceaseless worriers extraordinary depression and inability. Inordinate stress or continuous dread or tension is unsafe when it turns out to be nonsensical to the point that you can't concentrate on the real world or think unmistakably. Individuals with high tension experience issues shaking their stresses. At the point when that occurs, they may encounter genuine physical side effects.

Could Excessive Worry and Anxiety Cause a Stress Response?

Stress originates from the requests and weights what we experience every day. Long lines at the supermarket, heavy traffic, a telephone ringing constant, or an interminable sickness are instances of things that can cause weight every day. At the point when stresses and tension become extreme, odds are you'll trigger the stress reaction.

There are two components to the stress reaction. The first is the view of the test. The second is a programmed physiological response called the "fight-or-flight" reaction that welcomes on a flood of adrenaline and sets your body on red caution. Sometime in the past the "fight-

or-flight" reaction shielded our predecessors from such risks as wild creatures that could undoubtedly make a supper out of them. Albeit today we don't conventionally experience wild creatures or risks despite everything existing. They're there as a requesting colleague, a colicky child, or a contest with a friend or family member.

Can Excessive Worry Make Me Physically Ill?

Incessant stress and passionate stress can trigger a large group of medical issues. The issue happens when fight-or-flight is activated day by day by unreasonable stressing and anxiety. The fight-or-flight reaction makes the body's thoughtful sensory system discharge stress hormones like cortisol. These hormones can support glucose levels and triglycerides (blood fats) that can be utilized by the body for fuel. The hormones also cause physical responses, for example:

- Trouble gulping
- Dazedness
- Dry mouth
- Quick heartbeat
- Weariness
- Cerebral pains
- Failure to think
- Touchiness
- Muscle hurts
- Muscle stress
- Sickness
- Anxious vitality
- Quick relaxing
- Brevity of breath

- Perspiring
- Trembling and jerking

At the point when the unreasonable fuel in the blood isn't utilized for physical exercises, the incessant anxiety and overflowing of stress hormones can have genuine physical outcomes, including:

- Digestive disorder
- Immune system suppression
- Muscle stress
- Transient memory misfortune
- Untimely coronary vein malady
- Cardiovascular failure

If that inordinate stressing and high tension go untreated, they can prompt sorrow and even self-destructive musings.

These impacts are a reaction to stretch, stress is just the trigger. Regardless of whether you become sick relies upon how you handle stress. Physical reactions to stretch include your resistant framework, your heart and veins, and how certain organs in your body discharge hormones. These hormones help to manage different capacities in your body, for example, mind capacity and nerve motivations.

These frameworks collaborate and are significantly impacted by your adapting style and your mental state. It isn't the stress that makes you sick. It's the impact reactions, for example, unreasonable stressing and tension on these different interfacing frameworks that can welcome the physical ailment. There are things you can do, however, including way of life changes, to modify the manner in which you react.

What Lifestyle Changes Might Help Excessive Worriers?

Although over the top stressing and high anxiety can cause an unevenness in your body, there are numerous alternatives you have do that can restore amicability to your psyche, body, and soul.

Converse with your primary physician. Ask for a careful physical test to ensure other medical issues are not energizing your sentiments of anxiety. Your PCP may endorse prescription, for example, hostile to tension medications or antidepressants to assist you with overseeing anxiety and extreme stress.

Exercise day by day. With your primary physician's endorsement, start a standard exercise program. Undoubtedly, the synthetic substances created during moderate exercise can be incredibly advantageous as far as upgrading the capacity of the safe framework. Ordinary high-impact and reinforcing exercise is an extremely viable approach to prepare your body to manage worry under controlled conditions.

Eat a solid, adjusted eating regimen. Stress and stressing incite some people to eat close to nothing, others to an extreme, or to eat undesirable nourishments. Remember your health when stressing pokes you toward the ice chest.

Savor caffeine control. Caffeine invigorates the sensory system, which can trigger adrenaline and cause you to feel anxious and jumpy.

Be aware of your stresses. Put aside 15 minutes every day where you permit yourself to concentrate on issues and fears — and afterward promise to release them after the 15 minutes is up. A few people wear an elastic band on their wrist and "pop" the elastic band on the off chance that they end up going into their "stress mode." Do whatever you can to remind yourself to quit harping on about stresses.

Figure out how to unwind. Unwinding procedures can trigger the unwinding reaction — a physiological state portrayed by a sentiment of warmth and calm mental readiness. This is something contrary to the "fight-or-flight" reaction. Unwinding methods can offer a genuine potential to lessen anxiety and stresses. They can also build your capacity to self-oversee stress.

With unwinding, blood stream to the brain increments and mind waves move from an alarm, beta mood to a casual, alpha beat. Drilled normally, unwinding methods can neutralize the crippling impacts of stress. Regular unwinding methods incorporate profound stomach breathing, contemplation, tuning in to quieting music, and exercises like yoga and judo.

Ponder. Every day reflection — rather than stressing — may assist you with moving past negative contemplations and permit you to become "unstuck" from stresses that keep your body on high alarm. With reflection, you deliberately focus on what's going on at the current minute without thinking about the past or future. Reflection diminishes hormones like cortisol and adrenaline, which are discharged during the "fight-or-flight" or stress reaction.

Have a solid informal organization. Interminable sentiments of forlornness or social disengagement make it harder to adequately oversee stress. Individuals who are cheerfully hitched have enormous systems of companions. They have more noteworthy futures contrasted than those individuals who don't, however, they also have a lesser rate of a wide range of illness.

Converse with an expert advisor. Mental guiding can assist you with managing issues that trigger unnecessary stressing. Mental intercession can give you adapting techniques that you can utilize either inside or outside other treatment programs. The advisor will enable you to recognize what sorts of contemplations and convictions cause the anxiety and work with you to diminish them. The advisor can help you by recommending ways that may enable you to change. Be that as it may, you must be the one to roll out the improvements. Treatment is just fruitful and you need to chip away at showing signs of improvement.

Contrast Between Worry, Anxiety and Stress

You will experience worry, stress or tension at any rate on some random day. Almost 40 million individuals in the U.S. experience the ill effects of an anxiety issue, as per the Anxiety and Depression Association of America. 3 out of 4 Americans announced inclination worried in the most recent month.

How might you characterize the contrasts between anxiety, stress, and tension? Which do you think you've encountered, and what techniques have you utilized for adapting?

What is Worry?

Worry is the thing that happens when your psyche harps on about negative contemplations, questionable results or things that could turn out badly. "Worry will in general be tedious, over the top thoughts," said Melanie Greenberg, a clinical therapist in Mill Valley,

Calif., and the creator of "The Worry-Proof Brain" (2017). "It's the psychological part of anxiety." Simply put, worry happens just in your brain, not in your body.

How Accomplishes Worry Work?

Worry really has a significant capacity in our lives, as indicated by Luana Marques, a partner educator of psychiatry at Harvard Medical School and the leader of the Anxiety and Depression Association of America. At the point when we consider a dubious or horrendous circumstance —, for example, not being able to pay the lease, or doing severely on a test — our minds become invigorated. At the point when we worry, it quiets our minds down. Worry is liable to make us issue, illuminate or make a move, the two of which are sure things. "Worry is a path for your mind to deal with issues to protect you," Dr. Marques clarified. "It's just when we stall out pondering an issue that worry quits being utilitarian."

Three Things to Support Your Worries:

1. Give yourself a worry "spending plan," a measure of time wherein you permit yourself to worry over an issue. At the point when that time is up (start with 20 minutes), deliberately divert your musings.
2. At the point when you notice that you're worried over something, drive yourself to think of a subsequent stage or to make a move.
3. Record your worries. Research has demonstrated that only eight to ten minutes of composing can help quiet fanatical thoughts.

Keep in mind: Worry is useful in the event that it prompts change, not in the event that it transforms into over the top contemplations.

What Is Stress?

Stress is a physiological reaction associated with an outer occasion. For the pattern of worry to start, there must be a stressor. This is generally an outside situation, similar to a work cut-off time or a frightening clinical test. "Stress is characterized as a response to natural changes or powers that surpass the person's assets," Dr. Greenberg said.

How Does Accomplishing Stress Work?

"In ancient occasions, stress was a characteristic reaction to a risk, such as hearing a predator in the shrubberies. Today, it's everything that prompts a conduct reaction, starting up your limbic framework and discharging adrenaline and cortisol, which helps enact your brain and body to manage the risk," Dr. Greenberg clarified. "Side effects of stress incorporate a fast pulse, moist palms, and shallow breath. Stress may feel great from the outset, as the adrenaline and cortisol flood your body," Dr. Marques said. You may have encountered the advantages of worry as you dashed through traffic to get to an arrangement, or arranged a significant task in the last hour. That is classified as "intense stress," and the surge wears off when the circumstance is settled (for example you turned in your task).

Ceaseless worry is the point where your body remains in flight mode persistently (normally in light of the fact that the circumstance doesn't resolve, similarly as with money related stressors or a difficult chief). Incessant stress is connected to health concerns like stomach related problems, an expanded danger of coronary illness, and a debilitation of the safe framework.

Three Things to Help with Your Stress:

1. Work out. This is a path for your body to recoup from the expansion of adrenaline and cortisol.
2. Get clear with what you can and can't control. At that point, center your vitality on what you can control and acknowledge what you can't.
3. Try not to contrast your stress and any other person's stress. Various individuals react to upsetting circumstances.

Keep in mind: Stress is a natural reaction that is a typical piece of our lives.

What Is Anxiety?

Stress is the side effects, anxiety is the climax. Anxiety has an intellectual component (stress) and a physiological reaction (stress), which implies that we experience tension in both our psyche and our body. "Here and there," Dr. Marques stated, "anxiety is the thing that happens when you're managing a great deal of stress and a ton of stress."

How Accomplishes Anxiety Work?

Recall how stress is a characteristic reaction to a danger? All things considered, tension is something very similar ... aside from there is no risk.

"Anxiety somehow or another is a reaction to a bogus alert," said Dr. Marques, portraying a circumstance where you appear busy working and someone gives you an off look. You begin to have all the physiology of a stress reaction since you're disclosing yourself that your supervisor is angry with you, or that your activity may be in danger. The blood is streaming, the adrenaline is siphoning, your body is in a condition of "fight-or-flight" — however, there is no predator in the brambles.

There is a contrast between feelings restless (which can be a typical piece of regular daily existence) and having an anxiety disorder. An anxiety issue is a genuine ailment that may incorporate stress or stress.

Three Things to Support Your Anxiety:

1. Cut-off your sugar consumption … and caffeine admission. Since anxiety is physiological, energizers may have a critical effect.
2. Check in with your toes. How would they feel? Squirm them. This sort of pulling together can quiet you and break the anxiety circle.
3. At the point when you're in an anxiety scene, talking or pondering about it won't help you. Attempt to divert yourself with your faculties: Listen to music, hop rope for five minutes, or rub a bit of Velcro or velvet.

Keep in mind: Anxiety occurs in your psyche and your body so attempting to thoroughly consider your method for it won't help.

20 Things Life Is Too Short to Worry About

At times my life feels like it's stuck in an unbiased state, like I'm stuck in a perpetual circle of presentation with no advancement. It's during these occasions throughout my life that I stop, plunk down, close my eyes, and reset my mind for 10 to 15 minutes. In doing this, I drop my purported "issues" from my mind and feel new and stimulated.

I'm a geek with an affinity for numbers and tech, so I followed my stresses as I discharged their hold on me.

Here are a few issues I wound up agonizing over regularly before I found how to think and pull things together. Life is too short to even consider worrying about any of these 20 things:

1. Bills

Demise and assessments are a long way from the main assurances throughout everyday life. You'll have your heart broken; appreciate the sun, the moon, eat drink, and be joyful — and you'll make some hard memories in existence without taking mindfulness of tabs.

Regardless of whether it's month to month, quarterly, or yearly; bills are determined. In the event that you overlook them, they just get greater, stronger, and increasingly ruinous. The thing is: we as a whole have bills ... and letting them run your life won't improve its strength at any point in the near future.

It's anything but difficult to state not to stress over bills. Everybody realizes it's anything but a smart thought to stress over them, however, when you're suffocating and have an insignificant or basically no salary, it's somewhat harder to keep clear of those bothersome bills off your psyche. Life is too short to even consider worrying about bills;

The certainty to stand tall notwithstanding inconceivable obligation is a totally extraordinary monster. I can guarantee you that losing your home, vehicle, link, gas, and so forth won't slaughter you.

Quit dreading your bills — you're letting them control your life.

Here's a Few Hints:

- Make a spending limit for yourself and stick to it. Put your financial limit over whatever else. This will assist you with improving perspective on your bills and how they influence you

- Cut immaterial bills. In case you're battling to make a decent living, cut a portion of your superfluous bills. Digital TV is probably the most effortless bill to cut. There's plenty of diversion alternatives out there, and regardless of whether you buy in to Netflix, Hulu, and Amazon Prime, you'll be spending less every year than a link bill

- Pay back any obligations to loved ones first. They're the individuals who will be there for you at the base, not your bank and service organizations

- Keep your guarantee credits (i.e. automobile advance and home loan) current. The exact opposite thing you need is to lose your home and vehicle. If you need to pick between the two, penance your home over your vehicle. In a most dire outcome imaginable, it's smarter to be versatile

2. Cash

Cash is the reason for and answer to the eternal most pointless issues. We need bread — there's no denying that — we simply don't have to permit cheddar to be the wellspring of undue stress.

Continuously recollect that cash is non-existent, and saving don't exist in nature. Since moolah is non-existent, the entirety of your stresses over said reserves are in your mind. Individuals do some weird things for paper, and I'll never get why. Material riches doesn't liken to bliss.

Rather than worrying about your inventory of coinage, give centering a shot the things that fulfill you. If you seek after a vocation that fulfills your craving for greenbacks, you chance winding up in a profession you loathe. Money won't take mindfulness of that issue, nor will it assist you with discovering similarly invested companions.

Individuals who seek after their fantasies and interests consistently have more satisfying stages than those propelled by plunder.

3. The Past

The witted-beef among us who don't learn history are destined to hear it rehashed again and again by the individuals who do. A large portion of humankind's rough wars were pursued in view of clashing convictions over what occurred before.

The past is critical to gain from, yet you shouldn't let it hold you up and turn into a weight. Rather, look ahead, and get over that soil on your shoulders.

We as a whole confronted snags from before. There's no compelling reason to run from or be embarrassed about what your identity is or where you originated from, however, don't let what befell you divert you from your own objectives.

Gain from your hardships, and battle harder next time. The main way you can keep being hurt by something that previously happened is in the event that you let it.

4. Gossips

Gossip is exceedingly terrible. I wouldn't fret conversing with my companions or accomplice about what's happening in their lives, yet I'm uninterested in catching wind of everybody's own lives.

What are you picking up — a friendly exchange? You'll wind up seeming like the work tattle, who no one prefers nor trusts.

Rather than joining the grapes on the vine, stress over you.

While we're regarding the matter, there's actually no requirement for everybody to think about your own life either. It shouldn't be in your collection of ice-breaking discussion feed.

Life's simply too short to even consider worrying about what others are doing.

5. Haters

Consider all the big names you don't quite care for or just couldn't care less about: Kim Kardashian should not be acclaimed, Justin Bieber is exaggerated, and LeBron James is no Michael Jordan ... regardless of how you feel about any of these individuals, they have effective vocations.

In spite of the fact they get a lot of hateful mail, effective individuals keep doing what they're doing. Presently apply this idea to your own life.

Individuals aren't continually going to like what you do; there's hatred in the water. Regardless of whether you're a nearby big name or a virtual obscure, you're going to step on certain toes.

I've met individuals who are unquestionably the kindest, merciful, generally keen, and affable people, but they STILL have had haters state and do probably the most abhorrent things to them. In the event that I halted and worried each time somebody wasn't mindful of my choices, I'd never have achieved anything throughout everyday life.

Try not to stretch the haters.

6. Work

There will consistently be ventures, tasks, and crises of busy working. No one has a life without any upsetting circumstances. It assists with cherishing what you do, yet regardless of whether you don't, work is a senseless thing to get edgy about.

In case you're not busy working, there's nothing to stress over. In the event that you're grinding away, at that point quit crying over spilt milk, focus in, and be beneficial. The less you stress over work, the speedier it passes by, and you'll never be embarrassed about what your identity is or what you do to win a living. You're not character- ized by your vocation; you characterize it.

7. Maturing

Getting old is a troublesome and unnerving undertaking — there's no denying that. We as a whole experience a similar stress, anxiety, dread, and uncertainty. It's reasonable to feel somewhat worried about maturing, however, you need to remember there's no way around it. You're going to age in any case.

There's nothing you can do to stop the procedure, yet you can grasp it and capitalize on your time.

Maturing is a piece of life. Rather than agonizing over your looming geriatric state, appreciate the current you that exists in the present moment. You'll just be this old once, so do all the enjoyable things you constantly need to do at that age. Quit wanting to be more youthful.

Try not to burn through your time agonizing over not being mature enough yet either. Being youthful has its focal points. You get little disciplines for committing errors at school or at home, affirmation costs are less expensive, and bills are generally free. You can't speed or moderate time. Make the most out of life.

8. Death

At some point or another in your life, you will need to confront the certainty of your own passing. You can't evade the harvester of souls, and stowing away is just going to ruin you from carrying on with your life without limit. You won't give your all when you're keeping down.

After you face demise, you'll see it in simpler terms and look again and again all through life. You'll have more mental fortitude and industriousness.

Demise isn't anything but a difficult thing to confront; religions have produced all through mankind's history trying to alleviate individuals' feelings of trepidation of insensibility. In the event that you rest, you may not wake up, and regardless of whether you do awaken, regardless of how safe you are, we could be nuked by another nation or a meteor could drop out the sky and murder all of us.

Except if you're perusing this from an expert safe house, you get no opportunity of enduring an annihilation level occasion. Presently face mortality, and go carry on with your life.

9. What People Think

At the point when I was more youthful, I generally said I couldn't have cared less about what individuals thought of me, however, the fact of the matter is totally different. In my late 20s, I began to discover my enthusiasm and what I'd love to accomplish for my life. So, I began being me, paying little mind to what my companions or family pondered.

Fitting in is a bit of leeway in specific circumstances, yet it's unquestionably not the end. Be totally supportive of each circumstance throughout everyday life. There are times when you have to stay under the radar, yet generally, except if you're a mystery operator or political pioneer, don't hesitate to do what satisfies you, paying little mind to what individuals consider you.

10. Big Names

Paparazzi follow big names wherever they go, snapping pictures, recordings, and sound nibbles to take the mindfulness of them to the tangled masses. They'd have no motivation to take pictures if there weren't crowds of individuals wanting to gain proficiency with the most recent big-name tattle. For what reason does it make a difference?

There's bounty going on the planet outside the lives of famous people. Quit stressing over their dramatization.

11. **What Other People Are Doing**

It's not simply big names — a few people get into everybody's matter of fact. What would you be able to find out about existence from others' doing the same old thing?

I remember the times as a child where I would state "however ____ is going out to see the films" as a method for persuading my folks to allow me consent to go. Their answer was a valuable exercise: don't stress over what others are doing. They're not taking mindfulness of your tabs or putting nourishment on your table. Their issues aren't yours, and there's no motivation to take them on.

In case you're continually following the case of others, you will never excel throughout everyday life. Individuals who excel don't copy their friends. They walk their own way and motivate others to take action accordingly.

Try not to stress over where every other person is going or what they're doing — center on you.

12. **Health and Comfort**

It's pleasant to have some place protected and agreeable to lay your head around evening time. Solace nourishments and our customary range of familiarity are significant parts of our life, and it's hard to feel great in case you're undependable. This is the reason some part of security and solace is fundamental.

You can't get excessively agreeable in that shell. At some point or another, you will need to break out of your customary range of familiarity and experience life.

Taking risks is significant throughout everyday life. If you never take risks, you'll never go to bat for yourself, and you'll likely not have a fabulous time.

Rather than being tame and thoughtful, quit stressing over living to be 100, and begin agonizing over having a tad of fun. All things considered, you just live once.

13. **Errors**

Try not to stress a lot of when you commit an error — no one's ideal. At the point when you commit an error (particularly a string of them), it's anything but difficult to get baffled and feel like everything is self-destructing. Stress can compound as you race toward cut-off times, and the suspicion to quit begins to develop inside.

It's alright. You may need to pay a type of revenge for your error, however, that doesn't execute you and just offers you a chance to demonstrate who you truly are.

Make sense of what caused the misstep and what you can do next time to stay away from it or improve the result in some minor manner. Recall the thing Thomas Edison said about slip-ups being the way to advancement; we discovered a portion of our most prominent innovations unintentionally. It's not the apocalypse.

14. **Your Luck**

There's nothing amiss with periodically tossing a few dollars down on the lottery needing to win one. Somebody needs to win, and it might be you. In any case, you're not trusting that this significant minute will happen in your life before making a move. For what reason would you sit tight for some non-existent (and exceptionally impossible) godsend before giving life your everything?

While it's alright to play the lottery, don't place every one of your chips into that. Try not to rely upon the lottery, or some other impossible outside factor to come swoop you away from your life — work with what you have.

By seeking after your fantasies and objectives, you won't need to stress over the lottery; you'll feel like you previously won.

15. **What Can Go Wrong**

I'm not going to head to the store today. I may come up short on gas, traffic will be occupied, the store's most likely shut or swarmed, they won't have the thing I'm searching for or it'll be excessively costly, I'll overlook my wallet, my vehicle will get hit in the parking garage, somebody may shoot up the store while I'm there, my vehicle will stall, I'll lose my key, and my home will get burglarized while I'm gone ...

On account of these conceivable outcomes, I will sit home the entire day and do nothing.

In the event that you don't begin something since you're frightened of the considerable number of things that may turn out badly, you're presumably happier since you can't be effective and you don't have the foggiest idea with how to respond when confronted with diffi-culty.

Regardless of how well you make your arrangements, something will turn out badly.

Quit letting what may turn out badly prevent you from doing what may go right. Begin taking activities and quit stalling.

16. Stressing

Sooner or later, your stresses begin to accumulate to the point that you start to try and stress over stressing. When you're stuck right now, it's hard to get out.

In spite of the fact that you're in an ideal situation of not doing it, there's nothing amiss with stressing — stressing over stressing is a decent sign you have to stop and pause for a moment.

If you ever wind up like that right now, first thing you have to recall is to relax.

Presently quit getting baffled with yourself.

If life is too short to even think about worrying about death, it's posi-tively too short to even consider beating yourself up over being hu-man and having a characteristic response.

17. The Price Tag

Cost isn't all that matters. Stress over the strength and estimation of the item you're getting. McDonald's dollar menu won't cut it when you're in the state of mind for a decent steak.

I prefer not to sound middle class, however, strength is a significant viewpoint throughout everyday life.

If you need an extremely pleasant coat, buckle down, sell a couple of things, and set aside the cash to purchase the one you truly need as opposed to making due with an item you're not content with essentially if it's less expensive.

18. The Small Stuff

Try not to sweat the little stuff. Easily overlooked details turn out badly and consistently in our lives.

You woke up late, a dollar short for your lunch, got sprinkled by a vehicle strolling through the parking garage, entangled going up the stairs, and your zipper was down for an extremely significant gathering …

If you look at that as a terrible day, you're chronicling your life the wrong way.

Rather than getting baffled by the seemingly insignificant details, center on all the positives. The dusk, cloud arrangements, the smell of the trees and blossoms around you, nourishment, drinks, love, and enthusiasm — there are such a large number of extraordinary things occurring on an everyday premise to stress over the little inconveniences throughout everyday life.

19. Whatever Else Outside Your Control

A companion of mine's mantra when life gets too upsetting is, "this also will pass." I blend it up between "this is just impermanent." The general thought is to prevent yourself from getting irritated about what is beyond your ability to do anything about it.

I can't control the climate, the gas costs, the traffic or cataclysmic events. Be that as it may, I can control my own disposition and recognition on these things.

The most straightforward approach to lessen stress is to quit pondering on all the stuff you can't control so you can concentrate on whatever errand is close by — regardless of whether it's fortunate or unfortunate, concentrating on your present is the least demanding approach to either resolve or make the most of what's befalling you.

20. Being Perfect

Toward the day's end, you have to acknowledge yourself for your own issues. Life's too short to even consider dwelling on anything for a really long time except if it causes you to feel upbeat and satisfied.

Without a doubt, you'll commit errors en route, yet that is a piece of the good times.

Quit burning through your time attempting to be perfect. Test your own limits, and you'll start to appreciate life a lot more.

Inquiries to Pose to Yourself When Thoughts Get Overwhelming

"You can't transform anything by stressing."

What are you stressed over about right now? What do you do when your musings become overpowering? In the event that you're feeling stressed or overpowered for reasons unknown, dread will expand that feeling. You'll start to feel on edge and frightened on the grounds that your psyche is wherever it is in this very moment.

How Feeling Worried Affected Me

For me, I was feeling stressed over numerous things. I was stressed over my capricious future — consider the possibility that I don't arrive at my profession objective; imagine a scenario where I don't discover my life reason; will my child be tormented in school as was I.

I would feel stressed over my past decisions might I be able to improve; imagine a scenario where I had picked that rather than this; consider the possibility that I never change myself.

What's more, I would stress over others' assessment of me. I was stressed over my present circumstance in my life. I was feeling stressed; like being on a consistent roller-coaster ride with my own perspective.

The Way Feeling Worried Affected My Physical Body

Stress started to be reflected in my physical body. I had stomach torments, the tricky skin, and dust sensitivity. Also, the more physical agony I had, the more anxiety I experienced. The stress demonstrated its hooks by giving me circumstances that made negative results.

In any case, I didn't have the foggiest idea how to quit stressing. I had a few enthusiastic breakdowns since I was unable to quit feeling stressed.

In the long run, the stress started to show as anxiety. Until one day I said to myself, "This must reach a conclusion." I started to look for valuable approaches to manage my dim musings.

How Deep Breathing and Relaxation Techniques Helped

In that time of my life, I discovered profound breathing as a supportive technique. I've been working on being right now from that point forward.

Unwinding is troublesome, I know, however, it's simply the most ideal approach to deal with oneself. It helped me to change my predominant vibration. Unwinding in a type of profound breathing, being peaceful, going into a perspective without any contemplations, and turning out to be mindful.

Mindfulness gives you the clearness to concentrate on managing anxiety by tolerating it's inside you. You don't battle against it; you simply become mindful that you feel stressed and on edge.

At the point when you're mindful, you're prepared to locate the correct solutions to your stresses and you'll start to perceive the reason for your dread and anxiety. You simply need to pose the correct inquiries.

10 Questions to Ask Yourself When Thoughts Get Overwhelming

1. What is it That I Feel Stressed Over as of Now?

More often than not, you're stressing about the things that won't occur in the manner you need it to. It's the ego's requirement for controlling others. In any case, recollect that you can't control anything aside from your musings.

You can't make your life to be flawless on the grounds that it's ideal only for being blemished.

Stress is an inventive idea over things that didn't occur yet or won't ever occur.

So, imagine a scenario where things don't occur the manner in which you need them to. Do you lose yourself and your life? Of course not!

You should acknowledge what you can't change and proceed onward.

2. **Did My Stress Assist Me with Taking Mindfulness of an Issue till Now?**

By what means can stress help to take mindfulness of the issue when it comes out of dread as a feeling? It can just build the issue. At the point when you start to stress, you amplify the circumstance in your brain, however, as a general rule, it's only a feeling.

You can't plan for the future by stressing. You're just getting ready for awful things and producing negative vibes. At the point when you dread awful things will occur, you're setting yourself up for that to work out as expected.

You're not destined to be set up forever. You're destined to appreciate and live now and not in some place in your psyche. You'll discover an answer for the issue when you escape your stressed mind and unwind.

3. **Does the Stress Make Me a Superior Individual Towards Another?**

You're not a decent individual in case you're stressed. You just speak to yourself as a terrible individual who wishes that all the awful things to everybody around you would suffer.

It would be increasingly helpful to discuss the mending of an individual who's evil than discussing the sickness. You're not a decent mother when you tell your kid that the world is unfeeling so he should be cautious.

4. Does the Stress Make Me a Capable Individual Towards Life?

By stressing, you show dread and weakness. Obviously, you must be liable for your life, yet in a genuinely smart manner, as a mature individual, and not an adolescent.

You stress since you accept, you're answerable for your life being like this. That is totally typical, however by stressing, you're getting ready for the most pessimistic of scenario situations. This implies that you anticipate it should occur and recall, what you expect, is what you get.

Presently, you might be anxious about the possibility that in the event you figure this as a positive and this doesn't occur, you'll be much more stressed. You accept that you'll baffle yourself since you were certain and the result wasn't.

In any case, it's significant you believe in the procedure and keep on propping that inspiration up. It will come around.

5. Did My Stress Become a Propensity?

In some cases, you're concerned that you're accustomed to feeling stressed. You're unknowingly doing it.

This propensity doesn't serve you and you need to transform it to conquer tension. Your new propensity ought to be founded on positive reasoning and convictions that will serve you.

Presently, with each new propensity you apply throughout everyday life, you must be understanding and relentless. I comprehend persistence is in your schedule when there are numerous and different commitments.

Attempt to take a look at the propensity for having positive thoughts as an apparatus for improving your life. The propensity for positive reasoning will build your self-esteem and fearlessness.

6. **Has It at Any Point Become a Reality Something I Was Stressed Over?**

At the point when I consider things, I was feeling stressed quite a while ago. 95% of them didn't show in my life. Rather, what was shown was the inclination of anxiety, franticness, stress, and physical torment in certain pieces of my body.

I endured all the negative feelings through pictures I envisioned. I endured things that never occurred, very similar things that my restless brain delineated for me to stress out about.

What I'm attempting to bring up here is that you can hurt yourself by stressing. That is the main motivation behind why stress isn't beneficial for you.

Maybe stress doesn't constantly show, yet you make the opportunities for it to turn out to be genuine.

Along these lines, stop for a minute and perceive how antagonism and stress makes tension which harms you. Watch it from a non-partisan side. You'll see how harming stress can be.

7. **If it Has, How Could I act in That Circumstance?**

I recollect one circumstance when my stress demonstrated its face in a reality. How could I carry on in that circumstance?

I was frozen and squashed. I went about as a defeatist.

It was a horrendous encounter and one of my most noteworthy life exercises. I discovered that I was ready to make my life the manner where I needed it. Contingent upon my convictions, the production of life will be sure or negative.

Presently I decided to make positive outcomes in my existence with new positive convictions.

8. How Might I Feel in the Event That I Wasn't Concerned?

Does the appropriate response "free" ask you to escape your stressed psyche?

You'd feel free and serene living right now in the manner you should live.

Feeling free is sufficient, a valid justification to quit stressing now, so next time, instead of discovering reasons to stress, discover motivations to feel free.

9. How Sensible Is It for My Stress to Turn Out to Be Valid?

Subsequently, your stress will possibly turn out to be genuine when you put feelings into pondering it. This makes vitality for whatever it is you're agonizing over to turn into a reality in your life. At the end of the day, the more you stress over something, the more probable that something is to occur.

10. Why Do I Believe Being Stressed Is Acceptable, and Not Being Concerned Is Terrible for Me and My Life?

You can't frustrate yourself if terrible things occur while you think decisively. You disillusion yourself by deduction. Along these lines, regardless of whether something terrible occurs, despite everything you'll see positive outcomes.

It's not inspiration that overpowers you. It's pessimism that doesn't give you the space to inhale smoothly. You're not destined to stress; you have recently gained from others that feeling stressed is the main thing that demonstrates you're a person.

Toward an incredible finish, we'll perceive how we burned through our time by stressing excessively.

Manage the Reason for Your Worry

You need to comprehend what stress can cause to you and your health.

Be distant from everyone else peacefully.

Ask yourself inquiries with respect to your sentiment of stress.

Record the responses to these inquiries.

Presently envision each one of those stressed thoughts getting genuine; your anxiety indicating its paws.

Will you say — "I realized it would occur, I was correct," and feed your ego with the idea, or will you think, "What have I done to myself and my life or the life of another person? How might I write this?"

Since you understand where your stress can lead you, don't allow this to occur. Forestall it. Find at any rate five minutes today and be in total quietness.

Dissect your contemplations and feelings, then ask yourself the inquiries from this article. Thus, you will start your excursion towards completing the steady trial of feeling stressed for the last time.

Step by Step Instructions to Stop Worrying

Is it true that you are tormented by steady stresses and on edge musings? These tips can help quiet your stressed psyche and simplicity tension.

What amount of stressing is excessive?

Stresses, questions, and nerves are an ordinary piece of life. It's normal to stress over an unpaid bill, an up and coming prospective employee meeting, or a first date. Be that as it may, "ordinary" stress becomes exorbitant when it's diligent and wild. You stress each day over "what uncertainties" there are and the most pessimistic scenario situations, so you can't get the restless thoughts off of your mind, and it meddles with your day by day life.

Consistent stressing, steady stressing, negative reasoning, and continually expecting the most exceedingly awful thing can negatively affect your passionate and physical health. It can sap your passionate strength, leaving you feeling fretful and nervous, cause a sleeping disorder, migraines, stomach issues, and muscle strain, and can even make it hard to amass busy work or school. You may take your antagonistic emotions out on the individuals near you, self-sedate with liquor or medications, or attempt to occupy yourself by daydreaming before screens. Constant stressing can be a significant side effect of Generalized Anxiety Disorder (GAD), a typical anxiety issue that includes strain, apprehension, and a general sentiment of disquiet that hues as long as you can remember.

In case you're tormented by overstated stress and strain, there are steps you can take to kill on edge contemplations. Interminable stressing is a psychological propensity that can be broken. You can prepare your mind to remain quiet and take a look at life from a progressively adjusted, less dreadful point of view.

For What Reason Is It So Difficult to Quit Stressing?

Steady stressing can incur significant damage. It can keep you up around evening time and make you tense and restless during the day. What's more, despite the fact that you abhor feeling like an apprehensive wreck, it can even now be so hard to stop. For most ceaseless worriers, the on-edge thoughts are filled by the convictions that handle both negative and positive convictions that you hold about stressing:

Negative convictions about stress: You may accept that your consistent stressing is hurtful, or that it will make you insane or influence your physical health. On the other hand, you may stress that you will lose all authority over your stressing and that it will dominate and never stop. While negative convictions, or agonizing over stressing, adds to your anxiety and props stress up, positive convictions about stressing can be just as harmful.

Positive convictions about stress: You may accept that your stressing causes you to maintain a strategic distance from awful things, forestalls issues, sets you up for the most exceedingly awful, or prompts arrangements. Possibly you disclose to yourself that in the event that that you continue stressing over an issue sufficiently long enough, you'll have the option to make sense of it? Or then again maybe you're persuaded that stressing is a capable activity or the best way to guarantee you don't neglect something? It's difficult to bring an end to the stress propensity if you accept that your stressing fills a positive need. When you understand that stressing is the issue, not the arrangement, you can recover control of your stressed brain.

The most effective method to quit stressing;

Tip 1: Create A Day by Day "Stress" Period

It's difficult to be profitable in your everyday exercises when tension and stress are ruling your thoughts and diverting you from work, school, or your home life. This is the place the technique of deferring stressing can help. As opposed to attempting to stop or dispose of an on-edge thought, give yourself authorization to have it, however, put off dwelling on it until some other time.

Make a "stress period." Choose a set time and spot for stressing. It time ought to be consistent (for example in the front room from 5:00 to 5:20 p.m.) and early enough that it won't make you restless just before sleep time. During your stress period, you're permitted to stress over anything that's at the forefront of your thoughts. The remainder of the day, be that as it may, is an effortless zone.

Record your stresses. In the event that an on-edge thought or stress comes into your head during the day, make a concise note of it and then proceed with your day. Advise yourself that you'll have the opportunity to consider it later, so there's no compelling reason to stress over it at this moment. Likewise, recording your musings on a cushion, on your telephone, or on your PC is a lot harder work than basically suspecting them, so your stresses are bound to lose their capacity.

Go over your "stress list" during the stress time frame. In the event that the contemplations you recorded are still troubling you, permit yourself to stress over them, however, just for the measure of time you've indicated for your stress period. As you inspect your stresses, regularly think that it's simpler to build up an increasingly adjusted viewpoint. Furthermore, if your stresses don't appear to be significant anymore, basically cut your stress period off and appreciate the remainder of your day.

Tip 2: **Challenge on Edge Musings**

In the event that you experience the ill effects of ceaseless tension and stress, odds are you take a look at what causes it to appear to be more undermining than what it truly is. For instance, you may overestimate the likelihood that things will turn out seriously, hop promptly to most pessimistic scenario situations, or treat each on-edge thought as though it were truth. You may also ruin your own capacity to deal with life's issues, accepting you'll self-destruct whenever there's any hint of difficulty. These sorts of contemplations, known as psychological twists, include:

- Win big or bust deduction, seeing things in dark or white classes, with no center ground. "If everything can't, then I'm an all-out disappointment."
- Overgeneralization from a solitary negative encounter, anticipating that it should remain constant for eternity. "I didn't land procured for the position. I'll never land any position."

- Concentrating on the negatives while sifting through the positives. Seeing the one thing that turned out badly, as opposed to all the things that went right. "I got the keep going inquiry on the test wrong. I'm an imbecile."
- Thinking of reasons why positive occasions don't tally. "I excelled on the introduction, yet that was simply blind luckiness."
- Making negative translations without genuine proof. You act like a psyche pursuer: "I can tell she subtly despises me." Or a soothsayer: "I simply know something horrible will occur."
- Anticipating that the direst outcome imaginable should occur. "The pilot said we're in for some choppiness. The plane's going to crash!"
- Accepting that the manner in which you feel reflects reality. "I feel like such a bonehead. Everybody must be snickering at me."
- Holding yourself to an exacting rundown of what you ought to and shouldn't do, and whip yourself in case you disrupt any of the guidelines. "I ought to never have taken a stab at beginning a discussion with her. I'm such an idiot."
- Naming yourself dependent on botches and saw inadequacies. "I'm a disappointment; I'm exhausting; I have the right to be separated from everyone else."
- Accepting accountability for things that are beyond your ability to do anything about it. "It's my deficiency my child got in a mishap. I ought to have cautioned him to drive cautiously in the downpour."

Step by Step Instructions to Challenge These Thoughts

During your stress period, challenge your negative contemplations by asking yourself:

- What's the proof that the idea is valid? That it's not valid?
- Is there a progressively positive, practical perspective on circumstance?
- What's the likelihood that what I'm frightened of will really occur? In the event that the likelihood is low, what are some almost certain results?
- Is the idea accommodating? In what capacity will stressing over it help me and by what means will it hurt me?
- What might I say to a companion who had this stress?

Tip 3: **Distinguish Among Resolvable and Unsolvable Stresses**

Research shows that while you're stressing, you incidentally feel less on edge. Running over the issue in your mind occupies you from your feelings and causes you to feel like you're getting something achieved. However, stressing and critical thinking are two different things.

Critical thinking includes assessing a circumstance, concocting solid strides for managing it, and afterward placing the arrangement without hesitation. Stressing, then again, prompts arrangements. Regardless of how much time you spend harping on about the most pessimistic scenario situations, you're not any more arranged to manage them should they really occur.

Is Your Stress Feasible?

Beneficial, resolvable stresses are those you can make a move on immediately. For instance, in case you're stressed over your bills, you could call your banks to see about adaptable installment alternatives. Ineffective, unsolvable stresses are those for which there is no relating activity. "Consider the possibility that I get malignant growth sometime in the not so distant future?" or "Imagine a scenario where my child gets into a mishap.

If the stress is feasible, begin conceptualizing. Cause a rundown of all the potential arrangements you too can consider. Do whatever it takes not to get too hung up on finding the ideal arrangement. Concentrate on the things you have the ability to change, instead of the conditions or real factors outside your ability to control. After you've assessed your choices, make an arrangement of activity. When you have an arrangement and begin taking mindfulness of the issue, you'll feel substantially less restless.

In the event that the stress can't, acknowledge the vulnerability. In case you're a ceaseless worrier, by far most of your restless contemplations are likely fall right now. Stressing is regularly a way we attempt to anticipate what the future has in store for us and as an approach to forestall disagreeable shocks and control the result. The issue is it doesn't work. Pondering all the things that could turn out badly doesn't make life increasingly unsurprising. Concentrating on the most pessimistic scenario situations will just shield you from getting a charge out of the beneficial things you have in the present. To quit stressing, handle your requirement for conviction and quick answers.

- Do you anticipate how terrible things will happen in light of the fact that they are questionable? What is the probability they will?

- Given the probability is low, is it conceivable to live with the little possibility that something negative may occur

- Ask your loved ones how they adapt to vulnerability in explicit circumstances. Might you be able to do the same?

- Tune into your feelings. Agonizing over vulnerability is regularly an approach to keep away from disagreeable feelings. Yet, by tuning into your feelings you can begin to acknowledge your emotions, even those that are awkward or don't bode well

Tip 4: **Interrupt the Stress Cycle**

If you stress unnecessarily, it can appear as though negative contemplations are going through your mind with an unending rehash. You may feel like you're spiraling wild, going insane, or going to wear out under the heaviness of this anxiety. Yet, there are steps you can take to intrude on each one of those on-edge thoughts and give yourself a break from tireless stressing.

Get up and get going. Exercise is a characteristic and a viable anti-anxiety treatment since it discharges endorphins which relieves tension and stress, boosts energy, and enhances your sense of health. More importantly, by really focusing on how your body feels as you move, you can interrupt the constant flow of worries running through your head. Pay attention to the sensation of your feet hitting the ground as you walk, run, or dance, the rhythm of your breathing, or the feeling of the sun or wind on your skin.

- Take a yoga or Tai Chi class. By focusing your mind on your movements and breathing, practicing yoga or Tai Chi keeps your attention on the present, helping to clear your mind and lead to a relaxed state

- Meditation works by switching your focus from worrying about the future or dwelling on the past to what's happening right now. By being fully engaged in the present moment, you can interrupt the endless loop of negative thoughts and worries. And you don't need to sit cross-legged with light candles or incense, and chant. Simply find a quiet, comfortable place and choose one of the many free or inexpensive smartphone apps that can guide you through the meditation process

- Progressive muscle relaxation. This can help you break the endless loop of worrying by focusing your mind on your body instead of your thoughts. By alternately tensing and then releasing different muscle groups in your body, you release muscle tension. And as your body relaxes, your mind will follow

- Deep breathing. When you worry, you become anxious and breathe faster, often leading to further anxiety. But by practicing deep breathing exercises, you can calm your mind and quiet negative thoughts

"Relaxation techniques can change the brain."

While the above relaxation techniques can provide some immediate respite from worry and anxiety, practicing them regularly can also change your brain. Research has shown that regular meditation can boost activity on the left side of the prefrontal cortex, the area of the brain responsible for feelings of serenity and joy. The more you practice, the greater the anxiety relief you'll experience and the more control you'll start to feel over your anxious thoughts and worries.

Tip 5: **Talk About Your Worries**

It may seem like a simplistic solution, but talking face to face with trusted friends or family members — or someone who will listen to you without judging, criticizing, or continually being distracted — is one of the most effective ways to calm your nervous system and diffuse anxiety. When your worries start spiraling, talking them over can make them seem far less threatening.

Keeping worries to yourself only causes them to build up until they seem overwhelming. But saying them aloud can often help you make sense of what you're feeling and put things into perspective. If your fears are unwarranted, verbalizing them can expose them for what they are: needless worries. And if your fears are justified, sharing them with someone else can produce solutions that you may not have thought of alone.

Build a strong support system. Human beings are social creatures. We're not meant to live in isolation. But a strong support system doesn't necessarily mean a vast network of friends. Don't underestimate the benefit of a few people you can trust and count on to be there for you. And if you don't feel that you have anyone to confide in, it's never too late to build new friendships.

Know who to avoid when you're feeling anxious. Your anxious take on life may be something you learned when you were growing up. If your mother is a chronic worrier, she is not the best person to call when you're feeling anxious no matter how close you are. When considering who to turn to, ask yourself whether you tend to feel better or worse after talking to that person about a problem.

Tip 6: **Practice Mindfulness**

Worrying is usually focused on the future with what might happen and what you'll do about it or on the past, rehashing the things you've said or done. The centuries-old practice of mindfulness can help you break free of your worries by bringing your attention back to the present. This strategy is based on observing your worries and then letting them go, helping you identify where your thinking is causing problems and getting in touch with your emotions.

Acknowledge and observe your worries. Don't try to ignore, fight, or control them like you usually would. Instead, simply observe them as if from an outsider's perspective without reacting or judging.

Let your worries go. Notice that when you don't try to control the anxious thoughts that pop up, they soon pass like clouds moving across the sky. It's only when you engage your worries that you get stuck.

Stay focused on the present. Pay attention to the way your body feels, the rhythm of your breathing, your ever-changing emotions, and the thoughts that drift across your mind. If you find yourself getting stuck on a particular thought, bring your attention back to the present moment.

Repeat daily. Using mindfulness to stay focused on the present is a simple concept, but it takes time and regular practice to reap the benefits. At first, you'll probably find that your mind keeps wandering back to your worries. Try not to get frustrated. Each time you draw your focus back to the present, you're reinforcing a new mental habit that will help you break free from the negative worry cycle.

Basic Mindfulness Meditation

- Find a quiet place
- Sit on a comfortable chair or cushion, with your back straight, and your hands resting on the tops of your upper legs
- Close your eyes and breathe in through your nose, allowing the air flow downward into your lower belly. Let your abdomen fully expand
- Breathe out through your mouth
- Focus on an aspect of your breathing, such as the sensations of air flowing into your nostrils and out of your mouth, or your belly rising and falling as you inhale and exhale
- If your mind starts to wander, return your focus to your breathing with no judgment

Try to meditate three or four times per week for ten minutes per day. Every minute counts.

More Practical Step by Step Guide to Eliminate Worry

Method 1 of 5: Keeping a Worry Diary

1. Identifying Worry

Know what worry is. You can't solve a problem if you don't know what it is, so the first thing to do is to learn what worry feels like for you.

Write down when you think you're worrying. It may help to start with writing down how you feel and what is happening around you as well as the thoughts you're having. Notice how your body is feeling. Are your muscles tense? Maybe your stomach aches? You can then go back and analyze what led you to feeling the way you did.

Ask people around you to help identify when you're worrying. Sometimes when people worry, they ask a multitude of questions and attempt to feel as though they know what is to come. Usually, people who worry will talk about it and their friends and family will know they are worrying. Having them point it out will help you learn about how you worry.

2. Separate What Is and Is Not Reality

Worrying lies in the unknown. It makes sense because the unknown can be frightening. There are a lot of "what ifs" wrapped up in the future. The problem with "what ifs" is that they may never become problems and you'll end up worrying over nothing. This is why worrying is unproductive. It's important when identifying worry to know if you are concerned about something that is actually happening or something that COULD happen.

Write down what you're worrying about. Circle what is actually happening and cross out what isn't happening but could happen. Focus only on what is happening because that's all you can deal with right now.

It is OK to plan and prepare for the future, but once you have done so, accept that you have done all that you can for now.

3. Ask Yourself If Your Thoughts Are Productive

When thinking about situations, it can be easy to get off course and start thinking about what could happen. When you're in a stressful situation, it can be difficult to know if you're on the right path of dealing with it because of your worrying. Asking yourself what you're thinking can help you get out of the situation. If it doesn't, you know you're worrying.

An example of this is dealing with a car that has broken down. You need to get to work, but have no idea how you're going to get there. You immediately start to think about how if you don't get to work, you're going to lose your job. You then think about how you won't have money to pay your rent, and you may lose your apartment.

As you can see, you can quickly unravel. However, if you focus on the situation at hand, you won't have to deal with losing your job or apartment. That can be quite a relief since you really don't know if those things are going to happen.

You love your children so much. You don't ever want anything to happen to them, so you take every precaution necessary to ensure they don't get sick. You stay up at night thinking about all the ways they could've gotten hurt that day. Focusing on them being healthy, safe, and happy will allow you to spend time with them, so bringing yourself back to the present will help you do that and end the downward spiral of worrying.

4. Write Down the Things You Worry About from the Past, Present and Future

Some people worry about the past and how it has affected them. Other people worry about what they do now and how it will affect their future. There are even people who worry about all their past, present and future. Write down your worries to give you a sense of catharsis and relief in the moment.

Use a journal to write down what you worry about each day. You may choose to do this at the end of the day or just jot down a worry every time you have one.

Use your smartphone and type in each one of your worries. You can use the memo app or an app for journaling.

Method 2 of 5: Venting About What Worries You

1. Talk to someone you trust. It can help to talk about what worries you. Choose a friend or relative that will see how you're feeling.

Tell your cherished one that you're stressing, however, you have to get it off your mind, so you can proceed onward. More often than not, friends and family will comprehend and gladly be your soundboard.

In the event that it's conceivable, and discover somebody who has indistinguishable stresses from you, you can feel less alone in your stressing. You can then both work on quieting fears by concentrating on what you both know is valid.

Now and again stress is welcomed on by feeling like you are experiencing something isolated. Conversing with somebody can help offer you backing and solace.

2. Diary about the circumstances you stress over. Keep on composing until you can expound on it no more. This free type of composing can open a portion of the things your subliminal is managing. It may very well be astonishing to perceive what you record after multiple occasions, your stresses are enveloped with things that you truly don't comprehend consciously.

3. Address a specialist about your stresses. An expert can assist you with venting the stresses, process them and afterward let them go. Specialists understand that stressing is a perspective that can be changed. You simply need to take a shot at it and follow the direction of your specialist.

Discover a specialist that has experience helping individuals who stress or have anxiety issues.

Tell the advisor you're dealing with dispensing stress, so you can be more joyful.

Try not to be hesitant to examine your stresses inside and out. Here and there, that is the best way to get them out and gone.

Method 3 of 5: Releasing Stress

1. Inquire whether the stress does any bravo. Since you need to think about yourself, you would prefer not to hurt yourself in any capacity. Stressing can hurt you, so help yourself to remember that. For the most part, when individuals can be straightforward with themselves, they have a simpler time relinquishing the stress.

2. Include your breaths. Breathe in through your nose and exhale through your mouth. Check your breaths since stress can be exasperated with high-feelings of anxiety, which will diminish those levels.

If you keep on stressing while you're breathing, permit yourself to consider it for a minute and afterward exhale it away. Utilize your breath to overwhelm the stresses from you.

Do the same number of breathes until you feel loose. A few people will complete ten breaths, while others will take in and out multiple breaths. You don't need to choose before you start this method. Permit yourself to measure in the event that you have to proceed with when you hit ten.

3. Allow yourself thirty minutes to stress. Figure out how to control your stress by permitting yourself just thirty minutes. When your thirty minutes is up, reveal to yourself that you have to concentrate on different things. It might assist with setting a clock so you're not enticed to stress after your time is up.

4. Utilize the idea of the halting strategy. As soon as you begin to stress, advise yourself to stop. The activity of advising yourself to stop replaces the negative idea. You can do it out loud or you can utilize self-converse with letting yourself know. Numerous specialists utilize this method to assist individuals with dodging negative thoughts. When a stress enters your psyche, advising yourself to stop can assist you with relinquishing it rapidly.

Simply remember this is a psychological conduct. It may not be successful from the start, yet after some training, you may simply have the option to render any troubling ideas speechless. These strategies work for certain individuals progressively over others. If you discover this procedure doesn't work for you, attempt care.

5. Condition yourself to not stress. Spot an elastic band on your wrist and snap it each time you stress. This is a figured halting and it can assist you with stopping troubling musings, at that point center back around the present.

6. Put something in your grasp. Studies show that individuals who utilize their hands are more averse to stress. At the point when you're

centered on whatever is in your grasp, you won't center on your thought process for a really long time. You might need to place a series of dabs in your grasp or utilize a stress ball. Have a go at tallying the dots, or pressing the ball in a cadence.

Method 4 of 5: Dealing with Yourself

1. Get enough rest. A great many people need seven to ten hours of rest a night. Since lack of sleep can add to raised feelings of anxiety, which prompts stress, it's critical to get enough rest.

If you experience difficulty resting around evening time as a result of your stressing, address your primary physician. Tranquilizers might be expected to recover your rest to become leveled out, and that might be sufficient to wipe out stress.

For the individuals who need a characteristic tranquilizer, consider taking melatonin. Speak to your primary physician before taking it to ensure it's safe for you.

2. Eat a sound eating regimen. The nutrients and supplements you get from solid nourishments can help decrease your circulatory strain and improve mind working, which can help with stress. This would then be able to lead you to stressing less.

3. Exercise. Exercise lessens stress, so you don't stress to such an extent. At the point when you are stressing, it can assist with going for a run since it's hard to be genuinely dynamic and stressful. Fiery action can also discharge endorphins, which can quiet you while giving you vitality to overcome the day.

- Go for a bicycle ride with a lovely landscape around you

- Go through a recreation center
- Play tennis with a companion
- Stroll through nurseries
- Go climbing through the forested areas with companions

Method 5 of 5: Meditating Daily

1. Begin pondering day by day. Studies report that contemplation can calm tension in the mind. This is on the grounds that contemplation has a quieting impact on the brain. Since stress is established in anxiety, getting your nerves leveled out can assist you with stressing less.

2. Sit with your legs crossed and place your arms down next to you. This loosens up your body. At the point when you can loosen up your body, your psyche accepts that as a sign that you aren't at a serious risk and it can begin the procedure of unwinding.

In the event that you can't fold your legs, sit in any position that is agreeable for you.

You can rest, yet be certain not to get excessively agreeable or you may nod off.

In the event that you sit in a seat, make certain there is a delicate territory around you so that you do nod off during contemplation. This can happen to certain individuals due to the exceptional unwinding they experience.

3. Close your eyes and focus on your relaxing. You have an internal quieting component — your breathing. At the point when you center on your breathing, you will see that you're breathing too rapidly. If you are, simply back it off by taking in and breathing out.

Take a stab at including your breaths. Breathe in for three seconds and afterward inhale out for an additional three seconds. Hold your breath for only a second or two preceding you breathe out. Keep everything gradual to unwind.

4. Concentrate on how you feel at that point and permit yourself to feel harmony. Focus on what is happening within you while you're reflecting. In the event that you feel restless, rehash "calm." You may pick an alternate word or even a sound, as long as it is something that quiets you.

If you consider something that stresses you, don't fend it off or you'll simply get on edge. Consider it for a minute and afterward let it go. You may even need to state, "Let it go ..."

5. Stand up gradually. To take yourself back to your day, open your eyes gradually, sit unobtrusively for a minute, and afterward stand up. Stretch if you have to and leave feeling loose and absolutely settled. Slipping yourself into your day will shield you from getting restless, which can lead you to begin stressing once more.

CHAPTER 5
EFFECT OF NEGATIVE THINKING

The Power of Negative Thinking

Pop psychology has informed us that we can't go wrong with positive thinking. But new studies show that assessing our impediments is fundamental to progress.

Lie back and picture life after your aspirations are satisfied, the inspirational masters used to state, and you'll bring that final product closer to the real world. Put forth an attempt to envision everything about the completed screenplay living it up around your work area, the spouting audits in the paper, the games vehicle left outside. The masters asserted these pictures would electrify your assurance. They said you could utilize the intensity of positive deduction to will accomplishment to occur. In any case, at that point some significant research tagged along that muddied the ruddy picture.

Gabriele Oettingen's brain research lab at the New York University has indicated that picturing our points can reverse discharge. The positive symbolism can be motivating from the outset, yet it additionally fools the psyche into unwinding, as though the difficult work is finished. This implies that convincing the psychological scene of achievement, the more probable it is that your vitality will leak away. In the investigation, volunteers felt de-stimulated in the wake of envisioning achievement in a paper rivalry. In another, members who fantasized about their objectives for the coming week felt less lively and accomplished less of their objectives.

Why Picturing Future Obstacles Actually Helps

A related issue with envisioning what life will resemble after we've accomplished our objectives is that it urges us to disregard the hindrances to progress that are holding us up. While the dream about our fruitful new design line or our future rec center fit body may give us a frisson of fervor, it also diverts us from the reasonable advances we have to set up to transform our dream into the real world. Obviously, you have to have an ultimate objective as a primary concern—reason and bearing are imperative—yet as significant it is to contemplate the obstacles lying in pause.

Gottingen's group call this system "mental differentiating"—considering how brilliant it is accomplishing your objectives, while giving due consideration to where you're at now and all the separation and troubles that lie in the middle. Envisioning our points can reverse discharge. Fourteen days after a gathering of mid-level supervisors at four emergency clinics in Germany inquired about Gottingen's gathering and indicated they'd accomplished a greater amount of their transient objectives than their partners who'd passed up the preparation, and they thought that it was simpler to settle on arranging choices.

That is another advantage of mental differentiating: by contemplating the obstructions to progress. It causes us to pick difficulties that we're probably going to win and abstain from sitting around on ventures that are going nowhere. Have a go—consider one of your aspirations, record three advantages of succeeding, however, then interrupt and think about the three fundamental obstructions in your manner, and compose those down as well. Experiencing this standard will help guarantee you to direct your inspiration and vitality where it's required most, and assist you with distinguishing it if this specific objective is a non-starter.

It's important that psychological differentiating works best as an antithesis to higher confidence and desires for progress. At the point when you're feeling certain, it guarantees your positive vitality is directed deliberately into the assignments and exercises that are basic for progress (In case you're feeling low and attempting to get moving on any task whatsoever, at that point this isn't the system for you).

Positive Feedback as a Multiplier for Progress

One situation when we're probably going to be flush with certainty and hopefulness is subsequent to getting positive input. In a later report, Gabriele Gottingen and her associates tried the estimation of mental differentiating in a recreation of simply such a circumstance.

By considering the snags of progress, it encourages us to pick difficulties that we're probably going to win and abstain from sitting around.

Many volunteers participated in what they thought was an examination concerning imagination. A large portion of the examination members were given bogus criticism on a trial of their inventive potential, with their outcomes expanded to propose that they'd exceeded expectations. Ahead of time of the principle challenge—a progression of imaginative knowledge issues—a portion of the members were then trained on mental differentiating: expounding on how great it would feel to crush the issues, and afterward expounding on the feasible snags to succeed with that accomplishment, such as wandering off into fantasy land.

The best entertainers on the knowledge issues were those members who'd gotten the positive input about their latent capacity and who'd performed mental differentiating. They outmaneuvered their companions who'd got swelled criticism just from enjoying positive contemplations, and they beat those members who'd gotten negative input (whether or not they, as well, performed mental differentiating).

Along these lines, whenever you get some positive criticism, don't lose your core interest. Entertain yourself a little—you're on target all things considered—yet in addition set aside effort to consider the deterrents that remain, and the handy advances you'll have to sanction to conquer them. The psychological differentiating strategy prepares for lack of concern, guaranteeing the increase in your initial win is duplicated into a long-haul achievement. What's your take? Have you discovered achievement in imagining deterrents when making arrangements? How could it work out?

The Toxic Effects of Negative Self-Talk

We as a whole have an internal pundit. Now and again this little voice can really be useful and keep us propelled toward objectives, like when this pundit advises us that what we're going to eat isn't solid or what we're going to do may not be savvy. Be that as it may, this little voice can regularly be more destructive than accommodating, especially when it gets into the domain of over the top antagonism. This is known as negative self-talk, and it can truly cut us down.

Negative self-talk is something that the greater part of us experience every now and then, and it comes in numerous structures. It also makes noteworthy pressure, not exclusively to us, however, to everyone around us in case we're not cautious. This is what you have to think about with negative self-talk and its impacts on your body, your brain, your life, and your friends and family.

What Is Negative Self-Talk?

Negative self-talk can take numerous structures. It can sound grounded ("I'm bad at this, so I ought to abstain from endeavoring it for my very own security"), or it can sound absolutely mean ("I can do nothing right!"). It might assume the vibe of being a sensible examination of a circumstance ("I just got a "C" on this test. I surmise I'm bad at math"), just to decay into a dread-based dream ("I'll most likely bomb this class and always be unable to go to a decent college").

The insights of your negative self-talk, or "inward pundit," may sound a great deal like a basic parent or companion from long ago. It can follow the way of normal intellectual twists: catastrophizing, accusing, and such. Fundamentally, negative self-talk is any inward exchange you have with yourself that might be constraining your capacity to put stock in yourself and your own capacities, and arrive at your latent capacity. It is any idea that lessens you and your capacity to roll out positive improvements throughout your life or your trust in your capacity to do so. Along these lines, negative self-talk can't exclusively be upsetting, however, it can truly stunt your prosperity.

Results of Negative Self-Talk

Negative self-talk can influence us in some really harming manners. One enormous scope study found that rumination and self-fault over negative occasions were connected to an expanded danger of emotional wellness problems.

Concentrating on negative contemplations may prompt diminished inspiration just as more prominent sentiments of defenselessness. This sort of basic internal exchange has even been connected to depression, so it's certainly something to fix.

The individuals who wind up being captivated in negative self-talk will be progressively focused. This is a huge part because of the way how their existence is modified to make an encounter where they aren't able to arrive at the objectives they've set for themselves. This is because of a brought down capacity to see openings around them just as a diminished inclination to gain by these opportunities. This implies that the uplifted impression of stress is expected both to minor recognition and the adjustments in conduct that originate from them. Coming up next are increasingly negative outcomes of negative self-talk:

- Constrained Thinking: You disclose to yourself you can't accomplish something, and the more you hear it, the more you trust it

- Compulsiveness: You start to truly accept that "incredible" isn't in the same class as "great," and that flawlessness is really achievable (Interestingly, insignificant high achievers will show improvement over their perfectionistic partners since they for the most part less focused and are content with work all around as opposed to dissecting it and focusing on what could have been something more

- Sentiments of Depression: Some examination has demonstrated that negative self-talk can prompt a compounding of sentiments of depression. If left unchecked, this could be very harming

- Relationship Challenges: Whether the consistent self-analysis causes you to appear to be poor and insecure or you transform your negative self-talk into progressively broad negative propensities that trouble others, an absence of correspondence and even a "fun loving" measure of analysis can take a toll

One of the clearest disadvantages of negative self-talk is that it's not positive. This sounds short-sighted, however, looking into has demonstrated that positive self-talk is an incredible indicator of success.

For instance, one examination on competitors looked at four changed kinds of self-talk (instructional: where competitors help themselves to remember explicit intentions for play better, persuasive: self-talk that keeps individuals on-assignment, constructive, and adverse) and found that constructive self-talk was the best indicator of success. People didn't have to remind themselves how to accomplish something as much as they expected to disclose to themselves that they're accomplishing something incredible and that others noticed it too.

How to Minimize Negative Self-Talk

There are various approaches to diminishing self-talk in your day by day life.

- Catch Your Critic

Figure out how to see when you're acting naturally basic so you can start to stop. For instance, notice when you direct sentiments toward yourself that you wouldn't state to an old buddy or a youngster.

Recall That Thoughts and Feelings Aren't Always Reality

Pondering yourself may feel like keen perceptions, yet your contemplations and emotions about yourself can't be viewed as precise information. Your thoughts can be slanted and subject to inclinations and the impact of your dispositions.

- Give Your Inner Critic a Nickname

There was at one time a Saturday Night Live character known as Debbie Downer. She would locate the negative in any circumstance. In the event that your internal pundit has this questionable expertise, you can let yourself know, "Debbie Downer is doing her thing once more."

At the point when you think about your internal pundit as a power outside of yourself and even give it a silly epithet, it's not just increasingly simple to understand that you don't need to concur, however, it turns out to be not so much compromising but rather more simple to perceive how ludicrous a portion of your basic thoughts can be.

- Contain Your Negativity

In the event that you wind up taking part in negative self-talk, it assists with containing the harm that a basic inward voice can cause by just permitting it to censure certain things throughout your life, or be negative for just an hour in your day. This sets a boundary for how much antagonism can emerge out of the circumstance.

- Change Negativity to Neutrality

While participating in negative self-talk, you might have the option to get yourself, yet it can be hard to drive yourself to leave a line of reasoning speechless. It's regularly far simpler to change the power of your language. "I can't stand this" turns into, "This is testing." "I hate ..." becomes, "I don't like ..." and even, "I don't prefer ..." When your self-talk utilizes delicate language, quite a bit of its negative force is quietened too.

- Question Your Inner Critic

One of the harming parts of negative self-talk is that it regularly goes unchallenged. All things considered, if it's a running discourse going on in your mind, others may not know about what you're stating to yourself and can't disclose how wrong you are. It's obviously better to get your negative self-talk and ask yourself how evident it is. By far most of negative self-talk is a distortion, and calling yourself on this can assist with removing the harming impact of negative self-talk.

- Take on a Similar Mindset as a Friend

At the point when our inward pundit is even from a pessimistic standpoint, it can seem like our most noticeably awful adversary. Regularly we'll direct sentiments toward ourselves in our minds that we'd never state to a companion. Why not converse this, and when you find yourself talking contrarily in your mind, make it a point to envision yourself saying this to a cherished companion. In the event that you realize you wouldn't state it, consider how you'd share your thoughts with an old buddy or what you'd like an old buddy to state to you.

This is an incredible method to move your self-talk when all is said and done.

• Move Your Perspective

Now and again taking a look at things in the long haul can assist you with realizing how you might be setting too extraordinary on an accentuation of something. For instance, you may inquire whether something you're resentful about will truly matter in five or ten years. Another approach to move your point of view is to envision you're working out and taking a look at your issues from a significant stretch. In any event, thinking about the world as a whole and of yourself as a small, little individual on this world can help you remember your concerns aren't as large as they appear. This can regularly limit the pessimism, dread, and direness in negative self-talk.

• Let's Assume It Aloud

In some cases when you discover yourself thinking negative thoughts in your brain, just saying them out loud can help. Mentioning to a believed companion your thought process can regularly prompt a decent snicker and sparkle a light on how crazy a portion of our negative self-talk can be. Different occasions, at any rate can bring support. In any event, saying some negative self-talk can remind you how absurd and unreasonable they sound, and remind you to offer yourself a reprieve.

• Stop That Thought

Just leaving negative contemplations speechless can be useful. This is known as "thought-halting" and can appear as snapping an elastic band on your wrist, envisioning a stop sign, or basically changing to another idea when a negative line of reasoning enters your brain. This can be useful with monotonous or amazingly basic contemplations like, "I'm nothing worth mentioning," or, "I'll always be unable to do this."

- Supplant the Bad with Some Good

This is perhaps the best means to fighting negative self-talk: supplanting it with something better. Take a negative idea and change it to something empowering that is exact. Rehash it until you wind up expecting to do it less and less regularly. This functions admirably with most unfortunate propensities: supplanting undesirable nourishment with solid nourishment, and it's an extraordinary method to build up an increasingly positive perspective about yourself and about existence.

10 Negative Thoughts We All Have and What We Should Think Instead

I used to be one of the most adverse individuals on the planet. I felt like life was a constant battle and I'd been given one of the most exceedingly terrible hands, however, what might I be able to do? This is simply life. Or then again so I thought.

I'll always remember the first occasion when I heard when I was conversing with myself, which straightforwardly affected each part of my life. We can be the cause of all our own problems and our interior discussion can be very restricting. Like the vast majority, I was incognizant to this in some degree with evident snippets of information.

To say I felt like I'd quite recently won the lottery once I truly got this, was putting it mildly. Why? Since I discovered the negative thoughts

I had, which weren't realities in any way, yet the willful constraints I was putting on myself had the ability to evacuate. In the course of the most recent decade, it was clear to me how the vast majority of us really have the same negative contemplations. Here are probably the most widely recognized negative contemplations we have as a whole and what we should think.

1. **Have You at Any Point Felt That You Weren't Adequate?**

At the point when we feel that we aren't sufficient, we will suffocate into self-uncertainty and pity. It truly identifies with a low confidence, yet in all actuality, each one is adequate. You probably won't have the right stuff or apparatuses to accomplish what you need now, however, you're positively adequate and deserving of what you want. If you have a $10 note, and it falls on the floor into a puddle of mud, does that $10 lose esteem? Obviously not! So, for what reason when do you feel that you lose esteem dependent on what you have done throughout everyday life, try not to confine yourself, since everybody is adequate.

New Positive Thought—I am deserving of all I want right now, similar to every other person.

2. **I Can't Do It**

'Can't' is one of the most constraining words that you can let yourself know. Henry Ford said, 'Regardless of whether you want to or you can't, you are correct.' So, if you reveal to yourself that you can't, you're sending messages to your psyche and brain that you can't, thus that will be your experience. Your psyche won't attempt you have just revealed to it that it can't.

New Positive Thought— "I can do whatever I set my attention to."

3. I'm Not as Fortunate as Others

This idea originates from holding a figment that others' lives are better and they're more fortunate and that is the thing that isolates you from them. "Great" doesn't exist, typically there is a ton of exertion that goes behind that apparent "karma." It is very dis-engaging to feel that you will never have karma and it is just false.

New Positive Thought—Good things can transpire as well.

4. I Don't Think I'll Ever

Whatever you accept will turn into your world and this is true. You shape your future consistently by the decisions you make. You can undermine your chances by constraining your thoughts. What might it resemble if you accept that you could do what you truly wanted and have the encounters you wish? It can't take mindfulness of business the first run through, no matter how much you try. Stop yourself before you've even given yourself a possibility.

New Positive Thought—I am certain I will ...

5. I Ought to Be Better Than I Am

Utilizing the word "should" causes one to feel short of what they are. How frequently do you wind up saying "I ought to be move cunning, increasingly restrained, progressively beneficial, and so on than I am?" Recall how you feel after a while? Not great I am certain. Or maybe set yourself objectives for the things you're not content with as opposed to mentioning to yourself what you "should" resemble or be doing. Make a move with things you wish to change and expel restricting modals from your jargon.

New Positive Thought—I am putting forth an attempt to change what I don't have mindfulness for.

7. No One Wants to Think About It

It may feel that you're alone at times and that no one wants to think about it, however, I am persuaded that there are individuals pondering you that you don't know about. Individuals do mind, not every person communicates their feelings similarly. It isn't a decent inclination that no one wants to think about it, so quit concentrating on that and expecting what others feel when you don't really have the foggiest idea. Change your focus to something that makes you feel better instead.

New Positive Thought—People are mindful about me.

8. I'm Not Shrewd Enough

This is an extremely broad articulation, yet numerous individuals will say it frequently and afterward feel awful about themselves. What are you not shrewd at explicitly? I bet you recognize a few zones that you are cunning in, you could, if you truly attempted. Not every person is smart and impeccable in each region and this is the thing that makes all of us person. In the event that you feel that you are inadequate in a specific subject matter, make time to consider and realize whatever it is that you need with the goal that you don't feel along these lines any more.

New Positive Thought—I am shrewd and I am contemplating to ace this territory.

9. If **I Don't Progress Nicely, I'm A Disappointment**

Holding elevated requirements for yourself and having conditions appended to your self-esteem on your exhibition isn't reasonable. If you don't attempt you will never know. You have to take risks in life if you need to get many outcomes. Try not to be terrified of fizzling, the genuine disappointment lies in failing what you have attempted.

New Positive Thought—I am going to attempt, I am not terrified of falling flat, that isn't what is significant.

10. **Worst Case Situation**

Thinking whatever occurs, is in all probability going to be the direst outcome imaginable. What might it resemble in the event that you envisioned the most ideal situation? Our thoughts are ground-breaking and it's entirely expected to utilize representation as a system to envision the most ideal situation. Regardless of whether you envision the most terrible or ideal situation, you're affecting your outcomes. Quit concentrating on what you would prefer not to occur and rather on what you need to occur.

New Positive Thought—The best will occur ...

We as a whole have negative contemplations every now and then, all things considered, we are human. At the point when most of your contemplations are negative, you are undermining your joy by the day's end. Our musings influence how we feel and, what we do throughout everyday life. Try not to constrain yourself or what is workable for you, ace your musings and change your outcomes. Whatever you think, you are correct!

The Most Effective Method to Change Negative Thinking

Negative considerations are hindering to our general well-being and prosperity. Sooner or later in our lives we have all experienced them, yet captivating in negative reasoning can prompt a lower personal satisfaction. Without mediation, you can wind up feeling miserable or discouraged, as consistently as harping on about negative musings that prompts restless evenings, strain, or uneasiness. Be that as it may, you can defeat these sentiments by testing your negative attitude, getting progressively positive, and concentrating on appreciating life more.

Testing Negative Thoughts

1. Recognize your negative considerations. The initial phase in defeating your negative reasoning is recognizing that it exists. Overlooking these considerations does you not help you harp on about them, so the two practices ought to be evaded. Rather than attempting to push these contemplations away, pause for a minute to consider them and look at how you're feeling in your body. Creating mindfulness and passionate insight as the initial move towards turning you to be more positive.

For example, maybe you are figuring "I will always be unable to carry out this responsibility." Recognize the idea and proceed to tending towards it.

You can also have a go at posing yourself a few inquiries to comprehend your negative contemplations better. For instance, you can ask,

"What feelings am I feeling alongside these negative contemplations?", "When did I begin having these musings?", "What's going on with me, or who was I cooperating with when these considerations happened?" , and "When was the most punctual time in my life when I previously began encountering these emotions and contemplations? What occurred during that time? Who was a major part of my life at that point?"

2. Pardon yourself. Once in a while, our negative musings are established in something awful we've done or something we've failed on. Recollect that you are human and that no human is great. Recognize your sentiments yet then pardon yourself for what caused them. Despite the fact that it isn't unexpected to re-experience blame, it is also fine to let it go.

For example, maybe you have been off on your eating regimen for a couple days despite vowing you'd keep it up. Instead of working to remain quiet about guarantees, recollect that you'll commit errors every once in a while, and that is alright.

3. Question your negative considerations. Increasing a superior comprehension of your negative musings might be useful. Ask yourself inquiries about the negative contemplations you are encountering to increase better comprehension of the issue.

You can ask yourself inquiries like, "For what reason am I having this idea? Is it profiting me at the present time?", "If this idea is made from a connection or experience, do I have the real factors to approve why I am having these considerations?", "Is this something I can change inside me, and how might I roll out this improvement to improve things?", "Am I harping on about these contemplations?", "Am

I having negative musings where it disturbs my day by day life?" , and "Am I ready to use solid adapting aptitudes to address these negative musings? Provided that this is true, what are these adapting abilities, and have I used them adequately? Or then again, is this a problem that is begging to be addressed it possibly needs help from an expert advisor or guide?"

4. Recognize your advancement. You may not be in the place you need to be right now and that is alright. Set aside some effort to ponder the advancement that you've made as it identifies with your negative reasoning. You will find that you don't give yourself enough acknowledgment for the steps you've made.

For example, if you are considered yourself as a horrendous understudy, think about the time your teacher gave you excellent grades on a paper or how you have invested more energy contemplating.

5. Set up an idea account. You may think that it's comforting to process your feelings by keeping in touch with them, so get out your diary and build up a "thought record." Write down the idea that you've had, how you're feeling, why you may feel that way, and the answers for dispense with this sort of deduction in the future.

- Recognize when the negative idea emerged
- Recognize the wellspring of your negative idea

For example, you may compose something like: "I had an idea that I am sufficiently bad and it caused me to feel pitiful. I feel along these lines since I got a terrible evaluation half a month back. Nonetheless, I have been concentrating lately and feel even more certain."

6. Consider the results of your negative reasoning. Despite the fact you ought not to stay away from your negative musings, you ought to consider what great things can emerge out of them. You will frequently locate that negative reasoning and yield any positive outcomes. The more you work out your negative reasoning, the more seldom you will encounter these sorts of thoughts.

For example, if during an undertaking you figure, "I can't do this," consider how that will affect your work. It will probably place a wrench in the works, so attempt rather than be certain and beneficial.

Attempt to divert your musings to a few positive considerations at whatever point you have a negative idea. For instance, in the event that you are feeling steamed at yourself for bombing a math test, at that point you may ponder the A+ you jumped on your history test, or how rapidly you ran the mile in rec center class a few days ago. Or, on the other hand, you could simply consider something important that you like, for example, your benevolent nature or your own style.

Building Up a Positive Mindset

1. Record your qualities and achievements. In many cases, we ponder ourselves or circumstances since we have overlooked or disregarded the entirety of the inspiration in our lives. Take a couple of seconds to compose two separate records, one of individual qualities and one of achievements. You will find there is definitely a larger number of things to celebrate in your life than there are things to mourn. At the point when you start to think adversely, audit this rundown.

2. Take up meditation or do yoga. Reflection and yoga are extraordinary approaches to de-stress your brain and discover harmony throughout everyday life. Yoga is an approach to include inspiration into your life while working out. Build up certain mantras to think about while reflecting or doing yoga.

These mantras can incorporate things like, "I am amazing and I am sure."

3. Encircle yourself with constructive individuals. There is an expression that says, "You are the total of the five individuals that you invest the most energy with." Remember that your companions affect you, regardless of whether you recognize it or not. If you encircle yourself with adverse individuals, you will keep on having a negative outlook. Search out and create fellowships with individuals who are glad and positive.

4. Record the things you are appreciative of. Notwithstanding having a rundown of individual achievements and qualities, you ought to work out a rundown of things that you are appreciative of. This will assist you with staying positive during troublesome or disappointing times.

Consider including things like your family, companions or occupation.

5. Create positive confirmations. One amazing approach to battle negative believing is to supplant these musings with positive ones. Work to build up some substitution considerations that you can think and ponder on when you start feeling on edge or pitiful. You can utilize your rundown of achievements, qualities, just as the things you are appreciative of to assist you with intuition in a positive manner.

You may make statements like, "I am a diligent employee" when you start to consider yourself with negative manners.

Getting a Charge Out of Life More

1. Live at the Time

In some cases, we can get so worked up with our day to day schedule, and in the hecticness of life, we neglect to stop and take in the pleasant ambiance. Exploit life's little minutes and don't let them cruise by you. In the event that your companions welcome you to go out after work, go! Get lost in some cases and investigate new territories where you can live.

2. Schedule Time Every Day to Just Chill Out

If you're likely to have a lot of duties to be mindful of, set aside a few minutes for yourself regularly to re-center and discover harmony. It's much the same as you plan out time for your classes or for work. You should set aside a few minutes for yourself as well.

3. Attempt new things. Try not to get so made up for lost time in your standard that you neglect to attempt things that you've never experienced. New encounters can improve your life in manners that you might not have even thought of. Enjoy your side interests and grow new ones. Evaluate another sort of nourishment or take moving classes that you've been wanting to learn.

4. Practice good eating habits. Nourishment are undeniably settled into our psychological and enthusiastic prosperity than we might want to concede. Rather than gorging out on unfortunate nourishments, fill your body with organic products, vegetables, and protein

to give it the vitality it needs to do all the things you need to do in a day.

Recollect that you can enjoy your preferred nourishments incidentally, simply don't try too hard.

5. Use humor. Life is even better and agreeable when you are snickering and chuckling routinely. Discover approaches to put more humor into your life with the goal that you snicker regularly. Watch comedies, invest energy with your amusing companions, and yet figure out how to chuckle at yourself. The less genuinely you take yourself, the simpler it will be to free yourself of negative reasoning.

Cognizant vs. Subconscious Thoughts

Napoleon Hill, the twentieth century pioneer of positive reasoning, when seen that, "The intuitive brain sees no difference amongst productive and ruinous idea motivations; (it) will convert into reality an idea driven by dread, similarly as promptly as it will convert into reality an idea driven by fortitude or confidence." That's the reason it is dependent for us to recognize the distinction among positive and negative contemplations.

What's more, the main way we can "observe" the distinction among "helpful and dangerous" thoughts is to address them to discover which ones serve our prosperity, and which ones don't. In the event they're gotten from a misshaped recognition we have of something we've encountered, or have been affected by a negative assessment or conviction of another person, at that point they will make our musings be "driven by dread", and won't serve our prosperity. Staying with the storm cellar similarity, that the intuitive resembles the extra space of the entirety of your recollections from the encounters you've had, both positive and negative. It's not until we dig further into our subliminal to discover what convictions are put away where we can start to get rid of what is negative (damaging), and keep what is certain (productive). Until we do, we will continually be at the effect of our dread based on the negative musings running in our brains.

Scrutinizing your musings arrives at your cognizant as well as intuition.

At the point when a negative idea springs up in our brain, it for the most part triggers a feeling similar to bitterness or outrage, and it's by scrutinizing these thoughts that you can discover why you feel the manner in which you do. Thusly, you dig further into what's put away in your intuition (and why it's there). This is vital, particularly if you have to get out a portion of those contemplations and let them go. You aren't simply skimming the outside of your musings. Defeating your negative reasoning expects you to go further into your "thought base": your subliminal. Except if you reach far in there, you're just putting a bandage on your negative contemplations and concealing them without tending to the more profound injury. You aren't getting to the base of them to discover why they're there, hiding underneath the surface and springing up during times of stress or mental turbulence.

The cognizant mind screens whatever thoughts emerge, and fills in as a channel to either acknowledge or dismiss them. What it decides to acknowledge or dismiss has a great deal to do with what thoughts appear to be helpful or advantageous for one's feeling of "self" or "personality."

So, in the event that you have an adverse assessment of yourself, you will take into consideration antagonistic musings to come in and "remain there," which your intuition assimilates as your convictions, and those convictions will remain genuine for whatever length of time you take into consideration. In the event that you've acknowledged them as your existence, the conviction that you're fat dependent on something somebody said to you about your weight quite a while back, and still hold it as obvious, it remains put away in your subliminal, and at whatever point you are in a circumstance where you need to show your body, as on a late spring voyage or on the sea shore in a swimming outfit, for instance, you might be inclined to feeling discouraged or restless while never associating it to when that contemplation was "acknowledged" as your world. You will have a "fixed" conviction about your body that it's bad enough since somebody informed that to you, and until you question and challenge it with the Says Who? Technique to discover that it's not your unique idea, you will be at the effect of it on numerous occasions.

The equivalent can be said for any negative conviction you have and are clutching. Sentiments of inadequacy or any sort of self-hatred doesn't simply show up out of the blue. Those negative musings that make those emotions are typically concealed somewhere down in our intuition, and are so covered that we are totally uninformed that they're covered up inside us. It resembles strolling around with self-loathing, and approaching your life, grinning to the world, while never telling anybody that there's a piece of you that holds yourself in scorn.

Whatever negative idea you let yourself know goes straight into your subliminal and remains there as a conviction. The main way a conviction can be changed is in the event that you change it on a cognizant level, which is finished by scrutinizing those convictions to ensure they are valid. That is, regardless of whether they depend on truth or essentially a "contorted" discernment you have.

That is the reason, whatever you let yourself know, particularly if it's negative, your intuition trusts it. Also, is there any good reason why it wouldn't, since you are the guard of every one of your contemplations and convictions going into or leaving from your brain? Whatever you acknowledge as genuine, so does your subliminal. Tolerating a negative idea like, "I'm fat" or "moronic" or "a disappointment," will be put away in your subconscious as a conviction about yourself. Until you challenge that negative thinking, your intuition will keep it as a fixed conviction.

For example, if you disclose to yourself something like "I'm fat," and need to get fit, your intuition registers and acknowledges that negative idea as a conviction. If you truly need to shed pounds, "I'm fat," can't spurring a gainful idea should you believe it; it's anything but a helpful idea that mentions to your intuition what you need to accomplish, or what your expectation is, but instead it's simply ridiculing and putting yourself down. You're undermining yourself even before you start. In the event that you truly need to get in shape, disclose to yourself you will and wouldn't joke about this. In case you're true in your craving, your subconscious will trust you, and hold that conviction as evident, and together your cognizant brain and intuitive psyche can work together to accomplish the ideal outcomes you need.

A couple of years prior supermodel Kate Moss caused a significant disturbance when she was asked how she was constantly ready to stay model-meager year-in, year-out and she was cited as saying,

"Nothing tastes on a par with the feeling of being thin." Now, you may differ with her assumption, however, she is a case of somebody who is ceaselessly strengthening her cravings to be thin. She opposes the impulse to revel in nourishment since she has implanted a negative idea as a picture in her psyche about how great it looks and feels to be thin.

Your longing and confidence in yourself to understand that craving should be indeed the very same, and if they aren't, you will send blended messages to your inner mind, which will store those blended messages as your convictions, and that is the very thing you need to keep away from.

A definitive objective is to have the entirety of your musings and convictions, cognizant and intuition, to be comparable and in sync so they can bolster what you need with clear expectations. At the point when they are clashed, it's critical to sift through our contemplations to decide the wellspring of the blended emotions we're having. Scrutinizing our contemplations is a helpful device in disposing our negative thoughts. Doing so encourages us distinguish and perceive the tangled and conflicting musings we have, for example, "I need to get in shape, however, I'm apprehensive I won't have the option to do it."

It's alright and even regular to have an idea like that, which joins a positive expectation with an uncertainty or dread. In any case, remember that the idea that will best get your longing underway is, "I need to get in shape." That's the one you need to concentrate on and rehash like a mantra on the grounds that your subconscious is turning in!

The second piece of the idea, "However, I'm apprehensive I won't have the option to do it" bolsters dread and questions the part you have to address and challenge.

It's also essential to ensure that whatever it is we want to do is upheld and bolstered with positive, certifiable musings. Simply wanting to accomplish something, such as getting more fit, simply can't get it going. Ask any individual who's made a New Year's goals! You need to proceed with your psychological control by remaining engaged and watchful about not letting other blended or negative musings be a piece of your reasoning procedure when you need to arrive at an objective.

Let's assume you're attempting to stop an addictive propensity like smoking. It's one comment to say you need to stop, yet it's amazingly hard to be fruitful, particularly since smoking is perhaps the hardest propensity to break. Indeed, saying what we need to do is significant and a decent spot to begin, however, you light up a cigarette after you've chosen to stop and rationalize and reveal to yourself something like, "I'm simply having one after lunch and that is alright," you are plainly sending a blended message to your psyche that it is alright, and that won't assist you with stopping by any means. That is an ideal case of a craving that can't sync with an idea.

There are individuals who smoke who will even say, "It's a disturbing propensity, I know," and light right up. Despite how they might want simply to stop, if they're stating those sorts of opposing contemplations to themselves and think such words are unimportant and, in this way, won't meddle with their objective, sadly those words and negative thoughts will. It's much the same as letting yourself know "I'm fat."

You may state smoking is a sickening propensity, yet until you are genuinely appalled by it, and everything else you think bolsters your depression and nauseates with smoking, at that point stopping smoking will stay just like a craving you would like to acknowledge "sometime in the future." Unless you're letting yourself know precisely what you need to do gainfully and effectively—which I call an "Activity Thought"—at that point you won't have the option to arrive at your objective effectively.

Keep in mind, your cognizant contemplations and your subliminal convictions must be very much the same with the end goal for you to accomplish your longing. The most ideal path for that to happen is to challenge any negative ideas you've had, and expel it before it gets put away in your subconscious as a conviction.

We must be cautious that we don't set ourselves up to fall flat with our positive reasoning, which is the why it's so imperative to be clear about our cognizant contemplations, and the message they're sending to our subconscious. Once in a while our objectives are set so high that we make it practically inconceivable for ourselves to contact them, which is one reason those feared by New Year's goals never appear to work out.

Getting thinner is a genuine guide to depict the dissatisfaction numerous individuals feel about not having the option to achieve what they set out to do. The principal thing somebody will say when they need to get in shape is the quantity of pounds they need to drop, which is fine, and can be useful for objective setting. In any case, the number they append to their objective to get more fit can turn out to be so overwhelming over time, that their contemplations about getting more fit begins to debilitate and their craving and best goals can't hold up or continue itself under the heaviness of their negative reasoning, and they find themselves incapable to arrive at the number they declared they would.

"I will shed fifty pounds!" a customer reported with enormous eagerness to me one day. This happens a lot when people find energy and report another objective. Her energy, in any case, was more about the number and final product than the everyday duty it takes to really lose the weight. In this way, as the days proceeded, her energy started to wear off, and the thoughts that are expected to help her "want" to get in shape started to evaporate, and the "conviction" in herself to get thinner, particularly the quantity of pounds she'd put in her psyche, was no longer there. However, this was supplanted by negative musings of uncertainty. The issue with that kind of reasoning is that you're not just left with not understanding your objective, as my customer seemed to be, yet you may even be a host to ridicule, for example, "I'm a washout," which just worsens the disgrace and affirms a negative subliminal conviction.

The key is, when the primary negative idea springs up, to scrutinize that idea. Ask yourself, "Says who? Who says I'm a washout?" Doing so permits you to look at it and hold it up to the light of day. Except if you question a negative conviction you have about yourself or another person, or what something somebody has said about you, it turns into a lasting piece of your reasoning. Keep in mind, your intuition takes you, so in case you will broadcast an objective like, "I will shed fifty pounds," ensure it's sensible and you can adhere to it. If you have any uncertainty that you probably won't have the option to, why not simply start with disclosing to yourself something like, "I will lose some weight."

That's superbly fine and adequate, and if you do happen to arrive at your objective of fifty pounds or any numerous pounds you need to lose, you'll feel that improvement about yourself. The issue with being enthusiastic or over-requesting of yourself, and getting found numbers or measurements in your brain more than the everyday pledge to shedding pounds is that, in the event that you don't arrive at your objective, you can wind up feeling awful about yourself and return to verbally abusing yourself by saying, "I'm a disappointment."

Keep in mind, no ridiculing! Children do that in the sandbox.

The Origins of Self-Critical Thinking

A large number of our convictions are shaped when we are young and become our "center" convictions, which are simply the principle thoughts we have, and keep on having as adults. For us to work such that feels better or agreeable, we have to keep up with our constructive center convictions, which means holding contemplations like, "I'm amiable," or "I'm advantageous," or "I'm a decent individual," and so forth. Notwithstanding, given that we hold negative center convictions as well, and they regularly don't reappear until we're feeling helpless, furious, irate, hurt or focused on, that is the point where they can spring up as counter-beneficial negative contemplations in our brains. It feels like they have control or control over our reasoning, but as children we don't see how our musings become our center convictions, and we're entirely defenseless to being impacted by our friends and adults around us. We also need to be loved and acknowledged so it's simpler to oblige another person's feeling, regardless of whether we don't really concur or like it. So, the outcome is we frequently grow up with some pessimism in our conviction framework, and it can become unbending or even fixed about our specific thoughts or suppositions we have. It's not until you pose yourself as how an adult inquiries about a negative or dread based idea you have, which has transformed into a conviction, that you can recollect and recall who it was that revealed to you that you "weren't sufficient," or "weren't going to add up to anything," or something that was basic or disparaging that may have been said to you.

This encourages you to draw an obvious conclusion when your reasoning becomes your own. By doing this you would then be able to challenge this negative idea you've been hauling around for such a long time about yourself:

1. It's not your unique idea
2. You've heard it said by another person
3. You don't be mindful
4. Does not cause you to feel better
5. Does not work for you
6. Controls your reasoning
7. You don't have any desire to keep

An idea that doesn't serve your prosperity or impacts your life in a negative manner is regularly an idea that is dramatically overemphasized, mutilated and in this manner, not genuine. At the point when you challenge a negative idea that is genuine, you'll see it tends to be upheld with proof or truth, and known to be genuine dependent on the evidence. Be that as it may, suppose you can back up an idea with confirmation like you're a "frightful cook," or you're "terrible at sports," or "not great at math," with evidence (consumed meals or awful evaluations, for example).

The issue truly isn't your inadequacies or failures. It's the negative, undermining thoughts that keep on censuring you that do the most damage. Furthermore, that can be more harming than reality itself. That is to say, we all are acceptable at certain things and not very great at others. Such is reality. Be that as it may, it's the negative observation we have about it and the negative things we let ourselves know concerning it that reduces us and doesn't serve our prosperity. It's also how we decipher either a remark somebody makes toward us or what we inform ourselves concerning the things we see as shortcomings that figures out what we accept is genuine and what isn't.

For instance, believing you're a washout or unlovable can be a negative thought you hold about yourself that you've acknowledged you're bad or fruitful at something. Rather than tolerating that as genuine, you have to challenge those negative marks or verbally abuse yourself by asking, "Says who?"

By beginning with that first inquiry you are testing the negative thinking you have about yourself, which causes you to understand that since you may not be acceptable or effective at a specific thing, it doesn't make you a washout or unlovable.

The Says Who? Strategy

The Says Who? addressing strategy will start the procedure required for you to comprehend your contemplations better, so you can challenge negative reasoning when it springs up out of the blue and needs to undermine, harm, control, or shield you from being your bona fide self, and arriving at your objectives to lead an upbeat and satisfied life.

As I've stated, you can't lead a cheerful and satisfied life if your internal discourse is clashed or making you endure. At the point when you focus on utilizing the accompanying inquiries, and permit them to be your guide for dealing with your contemplations, you will perceive how clear and sharp your recognition will become, and how you can recognize and distinguish which of your thoughts are genuine and which aren't. By utilizing the Says Who? Technique with consistency, the primary concern will inevitably be, "In the event that this negative idea doesn't bolster my prosperity, at that point I have no utilization for it."

Utilizing the technique normally will give you the instruments to distinguish, challenge and oppose any negative reasoning that attempts to pull you down in a non-profitable way. It will empower you to decline to yield to the kind of negative thoughts that can make you mess up and crash you from arriving at your objectives. Says Who? Will assist you with remaining on course so you can make the inspirational attitude expected to arrive with satisfaction.

The Says Who? Questions

1.   Says Who?
2.   Have I heard somebody state this idea previously?
3.   Do I like this idea?
4.   Does this idea cause me to feel better?
5.   Does this idea work for me?

6.   Am I in charge of this idea?

7.   Do I need to keep this idea or let it go?

These seven inquiries will be the devices in your munitions stockpile to battle what can frequently feel like a psychological fight in your brain. Having them available to you at whatever point you need them will permit you to feel prepared to ace your psyche consistently. You will feel enabled realizing that you are in charge of your negative contemplations and that they aren't in charge of you!

Separating the Questions

By asking yourself "Says who?"—you are standing up to and testing a negative or dread based idea to discover what it's doing in your psyche. By replying, "I am stating this idea," you presently accept accountability for your negative idea, and can start the way toward addressing and looking at it while you discover what reason for exists for your prosperity. In this way, ask yourself:

Have I heard somebody state this idea?

You're seeing whether this is your unique idea, or if it came into your brain since you heard another person, for example, a parent, relative, instructor, life partner, chief, or anybody other than yourself express this to you. By distinguishing the originator of the idea, you can know whether it isn't your unique negative idea, and doesn't have a place with you as your own.

- **Do I Like This Idea?**

You're seeing whether this idea is attractive or engaging you. If not, for what reason would you say you are thinking it?

- **Does This Idea Cause Me to Feel Better?**

You're seeing whether this negative reasoning develops you or tears you down; improves how you feel or aggravates how you feel. If it doesn't cause you to feel better about yourself or improve your confidence in any capacity, for what reason would you say you are thinking it?

- **Does Accomplishing This Idea Work for Me?**

You're seeing whether this idea is helpful or gainful for you, and if it bolsters your wants or objectives. If not, for what reason would you say you are thinking it?

1. **Am I In Charge of This Idea?**

You're seeing whether this negative idea has any sort of hold or control over you, or whether you are in charge of it. If not, for what reason would you think an idea has authority over you?

- **Would I Like to Keep This Idea or Let It Go?**

You're seeing whether you need to clutch a negative idea that fills no valuable need for your prosperity, if not, would you say you will release it?

Except if you know the responses to these inquiries:

- Is it your own unique idea?
- Is it another person's idea?
- Do you like this idea?
- Does this idea cause you to feel better?
- Does this idea work for you?

- Are you in charge of your idea?
- Do you need to keep this idea or let it go?

… You are not always fully aware of your thoughts.

Question and Challenge Your Thoughts

No one is brought into the world as a washout or unlovable. Those are suppositions and convictions we develop into accepting about ourselves as a result of how we deciphered a difficult negative encounter we had or something somebody said about us.

"Says who?" is asking yourself, "Who says I'm a washout or unlovable?" "Did I reveal to myself that I'm a failure or unlovable?" or "Did another person say that regarding me?" You have to know that first before you ask yourself the consequent six inquiries of the technique. It's critical to assume liability for your negative musings, and you can comprehend that any negative idea you have is something no one but you can change when you need to. Furthermore, regardless of whether your negative idea or supposition about yourself was something you acknowledged due to another person's assessment of you, it is still dependent upon you to transform it in the event that you don't become mindful of it.

It's as basic as trying negative thinking with, "Says who?" and afterward catching up with a short arrangement of inquiries intended to decide whether your thoughts are serving your prosperity by supporting and asserting your wants and objectives.

We can reveal to ourselves a wide range of things we wish were diverse about ourselves: "I want to be taller, slenderer, more intelligent, increasingly innovative, progressively fruitful," and so forth. We all have things about ourselves we wish were extraordinary, yet it's imperative to know when those thoughts go into a negative assault mode over what you wish was diverse about you. There's a major distinction between having a desire or an assessment about yourself that is straightforward and innocuous versus connecting a negative idea to it.

I'm not saying that each and every idea we have can be or even ought to be sparkling and complimentary, however, since each negative idea you have impacts everything in your life, you should conclude that you need your interior discourse to be sure and profitable, which can cause you to feel great about yourself, and a smidgen of self-applause positively can't hurt. Trustworthiness about ourselves is a certain something, however, tearing yourself down is totally pointless, counter-beneficial, and fills no need at all for your prosperity.

Your Authentic Self

The Says Who? Technique will assist you with getting to the base of your negative reasoning so you can recognize what is genuine and what isn't. Consider it your fact indicator, or your compass highlighting your real self, the you that was entire and existed in a "genuine natural" state before your negative musings and convictions affected and contorted your view of your genuine pith, confidence, and sound picture of yourself.

It's an ideal opportunity to come back to your unique, bona fide self, and be available in your life as somebody who has the right to adore and acknowledge yourself for who you truly are, and intended to be. Also, if you're likely to change certain things about yourself you might want to improve, chill out with consideration, and not analyze the negative. You will get substantially more positive outcomes by urging yourself to be better at something, or as well as can be expected be by speculation positive musings that are profitable and steady. Your thoughts ought to be your cheering crew, not your hecklers.

Be clear about your longing, and the cognizant positive contemplations you let yourself know, which at that point gets put away in your subconscious as convictions.

In any case, simply becoming more acquainted with your contemplations and their starting point is just the start of your excursion of mindfulness, an excursion that will permit you to the end to have the option to perceive, comprehend and dispose of your negative musings better than you have previously, and let you control them as opposed to having them control you.

Challenging negative thinking will assist you with shaping a profitable connection among you and your contemplations, implying that it will yield a durable working framework where your musings are permitted to "consume" your brain. This considers you responsible for them, a significant advance that you need to be accountable for your thoughts. You should be the controller of what musings remain in and what thoughts go out.

In any case, with the end goal for you to genuinely have the option to put the Says Who? strategy to work and receive the best outcomes in return, it's essential to be totally dedicated to seeing how your thoughts work, and need to change the negative thoughts into gainful positive contemplations with consistency. This needs to turn into your better approach for intuition, which requires a psychological order. Much the same as you would exercise to deal with your body and keep it fit as a fiddle, or eat well to deal with your health, you have to deal with your reasoning, and ensure your mental health is in top conditions.

The first step, even before you utilize the Says Who? Technique, when a horrendous or negative idea comes into your head and takes steps to throw you off your base is to recognize it immediately.

Recognize:

Perceive its reality, regardless of whether it's upsetting. Try not to deny it or attempt to push it away. This permits you to perceive you're having a negative idea and admit to yourself that it is occurring. Being right now is significant on the grounds that it permits you to concentrate on what is happening in the "now," which is genuine, rather than the feeling encompassing the idea.

Doing this will help put you in the spectator mode, rather than responsive mode.

Onlooker Mode:

Watching your idea implies you are tuning in to it like an observer. This permits you to isolate yourself from your negative reasoning and be free of it. By doing this you are not responding to it or having it impact your perspective in any capacity, however, you're becoming simply mindful to it.

Responsive Mode:

Being responsive is something contrary to watching. Receptive Mode implies you are reacting to your negative idea without recognizing or watching it. At the point when you are in the right now mind you can't separate yourself from your negative reasoning nor would you be able to address it to see whether it is genuine or not. You are helpless before your negative idea and it is controlling you.

By recognizing your negative idea, and afterward analyzing it intently as a spectator and not a reactor, you can distinguish whether it is a beneficial idea that encourages you to work in a positive manner through everyday life and serves your prosperity or if it's an idea that causes you to feel awful or frightful, and fills no need for your prosperity by any means.

You would then be able to start the Says Who? Addressing procedure to discover what that negative idea is doing in your psyche and what it needs from you. Consider it a gatecrasher.

The equivalent can be said about a negative, meddling idea that springs up in your psyche out of the blue and is excluded. By being the spectator, you're applying a similar sort of addressing to your negative or troublesome thoughts as you would an interloper.

The primary thing you have to ask yourself when a negative idea flies into your brain is "Says who?" which signifies, "Who is stating this idea in my psyche and why?" This promptly builds up what it's happening in your brain and what it needs from you. This first inquiry will also begin the procedure expected to identify and challenge your negative deduction as genuine or not.

The resulting addresses will challenge your negative idea significantly more with the goal that you can get to its base and the expectation behind it. By testing further, you would then be able to choose if you need to keep your negative idea or let it go, but that choice is totally up to you. You're in charge of your musings.

By challenging a negative idea with "Says who?" you are requesting it to uncover who is answerable for this idea in your brain. As such, how could it arrive? When you discover the answer, you need to do something about it. Is it your unique idea, or was it another person's and you took it on as your own? You may even find it is an old idea that has become some portion of your center convictions, and now it's a great opportunity to challenge it and let it go.

CHAPTER 6
COGNITIVE BEHAVIORAL THERAPY (CBT)

What Is CBT?

I wonder, have you heard about "CBT" before? Well, if not, then let me tell you about it ...

Cognitive Behavioral Treatment, or CBT, is a typical talk treatment for certain individuals who can function to or be superior to drug to treat hypochondria. It very well may be powerful if your downturn is mellow or moderate. It additionally can help with increasingly extreme cases if your specialist is exceptionally talented. Now and again, CBT can help you the most on the off chance that you join it with different medications, similar to antidepressants or different medications.

How CBT Works?

An advisor aids you to distinguish negative or bogus contemplations and supplant those thoughts with more advantageous, increasingly sensible ones. For instance, you may feel useless or accept that your life is terrible and will just deteriorate. Or, on the other hand, you may fixate on your imperfections and inadequacies.

Initially, CBT makes you mindful if you have these musings. At that point it instructs you to swap them for increasingly positive ones. The adjustment in your mentality prompts an adjustment in your conduct. That can help facilitate your downturn.

You may get up in the first part of the day and say, "What's the purpose of endeavoring?" With CBT, you learn it to let yourself know, "That is not a supportive idea. Putting forth an attempt has bunches of remunerations. I'll begin by getting up."

You may require weeks or long stretches of CBT before you begin to feel much improved.

How Well Does It Work?

CBT is the best-demonstrated type of talk treatment like psychotherapy. In some cases it functions just as stimulant medications do for certain kinds of gloom. Some examination recommends that individuals who get CBT might be half as likely as those taking drugs alone to have sadness again inside a year.

Prescription functions admirably to treat discouragement. If you get a CBT, your treatment may work stunningly better and the advantages may last more. Many people who use CBT for discouragement or anxiety keep on continuing to utilize the aptitudes they learned in treatment a year later.

If you're taking drugs for melancholy, take it without conversing with your PCP first, regardless of whether you're working with a CBT advisor. If you quit out of nowhere, it can cause serious melancholy and different issues.

What's in Store?

You can get CBT from a therapist, authorized advisor, authorized clinical social laborer, or different experts with mental health specializations. Meetings can be one-on-one, in a gathering, or with self-improvement materials under your therapist's direction.

Your advisor will work with you to set treatment objectives to feel less discouraged or to reduce liquor. Typically, you won't invest a lot of energy concentrating on your past or your characteristics. Rather, your advisor will assist you with concentrating on how you currently feel and think, and how to transform it.

Treatment as a rule endures 10-20 meetings. A few people go only a couple of times, while others may get treatment for over a year. Your advisor may give you undertakings to do it all alone.

Before your treatment closes, your advisor will give you abilities to shield your downturn from returning. If it does, it's a smart thought to get treatment once more. You can also do it whenever you feel terrible or need to work through an intense issue.

Work with prepared psychotherapists. Their activity titles can contrast, and is contingent upon their job and training. Most have a doctoral qualification with explicit preparing in mental directing. Specialists, for instance, are clinical specialists who can recommend prescription and offer psychotherapy.

Before you pick an advisor, check their:

- Accreditation and permit in your state
- Specialized topic, especially if it incorporates in sadness. A few advisors have some expertise with dietary problems, PTSD, and different conditions. It's significant that you believe your advisor and feel they are your ally. In case you're awkward or don't perceive any upgrades, you might need to switch advisors

Cognitive Behavioral Therapy (CBT) can get you to out-think negative patterns that might be keeping you from sadness recuperation and from getting a better charge out of life.

Negative reasoning can slow wretchedness recuperation, and the explanation is self-evident: If you think negative musings, you're bound to remain discouraged. However, what's more subtle is the path individuals with melancholy arrangement with positive feelings take. Analysts have mentioned an astonishing objective fact: People with sorrow don't need constructive feelings, they simply don't permit themselves to feel them.

This psychological style is classified as "dampening," says Chloe Carmichael, PhD, a clinician in New York. It includes stifling positive feelings with thoughts like, "I don't have the right to be this glad," or "This nice sentiment won't last." For instance, another "mother with post pregnancy anxiety may reveal to herself she doesn't have the right to recoup since she's an awful mother for being discouraged in any case," Dr. Carmichael says.

For what reason do individuals with wretchedness think along these lines? Carmichael alludes to that negative voice as cautious cynicism—assurance against getting high expectations run. "You would prefer not to be the numb-skull, so you resort to hosing positive musings to shield yourself from potential frustration," she says.

How CBT Can Help with the Negative Thoughts of Depression

Cognitive Behavioral Therapy (CBT) has been found to help with hypochondria treatment. In CBT, you and your psychologist cooperate to concur on patterns of conduct that should be changed. The objective is to recalibrate the piece of your brain that is keeping such a tight grasp on cheerful thoughts.

"A sudden response to a significant life occasion may be at the base of the hosing impact," Carmichael says. "Through CBT, you and your specialist address it and work toward placing it into point of view."

Normal CBT meetings and work you do all alone outside of treatment can help strengthen the new patterns, "To have the option to perceive those negative contemplations and abandon them can be very freeing," Carmichael says.

5 CBT Techniques to Counteract the Negative Thinking of Depression

Carmichael has discovered that individuals with sorrow react well to self-study. Hence, she prescribes focusing on CBT for in any event a month and a half. Your advisor will show you CBT methodologies that can help check the negative intuition related with melancholy. She or he can also assist you with remaining on target with rehearsing the systems. Here are five CBT techniques you may wind up taking a shot at with your specialist:

1. Find the issue and conceptualize arrangements. Journaling and conversing with your advisor can assist you with finding the foundation of your downturn. When you have a thought, record in a basic sentence about what's troubling you and consider approaches to improve the issue. "A sign of wretchedness," Carmichael says, "is sadness—a skepticism that things can ever show signs of improvement." Recording a rundown of things, you can do to improve a circumstance can help ease burdensome emotions. For instance, in case you're

combating forlornness, activity steps may incorporate joining a neighborhood club dependent on your inclinations or pursue Internet dating.

2. Keep in touch with self-articulations to balance negative contemplations. Subsequent to finding the root issues of your downturn, think about the negative musings you use to hose positive ones. Compose a self-explanation to check each negative idea. Recall your self-proclamations and rehash them back to yourself when you notice the little voice in your mind sneaking in to snuff out a positive idea. In time, you'll make new affiliations, supplanting the negative thoughts with positive ones.

Carmichael says that the self-proclamation shouldn't be excessively far from the negative idea, or the psyche probably won't acknowledge it. For instance, if the negative idea is, "I'm so discouraged at the present time," as opposed to stating, "I'm feeling extremely glad now," a superior articulation may be, "Each life has high points and low points, and mine does as well." The message discloses to you that it's alright to knock up the level of bliss you experience. Simultaneously, your psyche commends itself for holding delight under control to shield from disillusionment. "It's alright to perceive that piece of you that is attempting to accomplish something sound," she says.

"In some cases, self-articulations become excessively normal and should be invigorated," Carmichael says. She prescribes to make an interpretation of your self-proclamations into different languages that you may speak, or rephrase them, perhaps in any event, knocking up their cheerful emotions a piece. For instance, the self-articulation "It's alright to investigate my ups" may turn into "It's alright to have a super 'up' day.

3. Find new chances to think of positive musings. Individuals who go into a room and promptly think, "I despise that divider shading," may prepare themselves to find five things in the room that they feel emphatically about as fast as they could reasonably be expected. Set your telephone to remind you three times each day to reframe your contemplations into something positive. Carmichael prescribes "buddying up" with another person dealing with a similar strategy. That way, you and your pal can get energized over having positive thoughts and encounters to impart to one another for the duration of the day.

4. Finish every day by envisioning its best parts. Toward the end of every day, record or type into an online diary the things throughout your life you're generally appreciative for. "Recording positive musings, and in any event, sharing those thoughts on the web, can assist you with shaping new relationship in your mind or make new pathways," Carmichael says. Somebody who's made another pathway of reasoning may go from getting up in the first part of the day thinking, "Ugh, another workday" to "What a wonderful day it is."

5. Figure out how to acknowledge disillusionment as a typical piece of life. Baffling circumstances are a piece of life, and your reaction can influence how rapidly you can push ahead. Somebody experiencing a separation may accuse oneself or even put on weight, thinking, "What's the point in looking great? I'll never meet any other individual."

A superior methodology may be to permit yourself to feel frustrated and recall how a few things are out of your control. Work on what is inside your control: If at this point in time of the book you have not done it yet, I really encourage you to write down what occurred, what you gained from the experience, and what you can do another way next time, keeping an eye out for excessively negative musings. This can assist you with proceeding onward and rest easy thinking about your future.

It's clear that our positive and negative musings impact everything in our lives. They figure out what we feel about ourselves, others, and the world, and what we express about our convictions, feelings, qualities, and decisions. Since our thoughts are shaped by how we see things, contingent upon our encounters positive or negative our thoughts and perspectives about everything depend on how we are influenced by those encounters, and however we decipher those encounters.

A case of this would be when you were youthful and somebody, an instructor, kin, companion, or even total outsider, let you know or gave you the feeling that you weren't "adequate" at something, be it singing, moving, school, ball, or whatever. Until that individual said that to you, or caused you to feel that way, you probably won't have pondered it yourself, yet since another person's idea has advanced into your brain, unchallenged, you've acknowledged it as evident. Except if you've had reason or proof in any case to challenge it, you've taken that conviction on as your own. That negative idea will stay in your psyche, regardless of whether it's driven into your intuition where you may be unconscious of it, or until a person or thing triggers it, and you respond to it genuinely without truly knowing why.

So, to comprehend our negative reasoning examples, it's essential to know how they work. Envision our psyche as having two levels to it, similar to a house for example, with the fundamental floor being the cognizant brain and the storm cellar being the intuition. This permits us to perceive how there are two pieces of our brain, cooperating and existing "under a similar rooftop": the cognizant and the subconscious.

The cognizant piece of our psyche is answerable for rationale and thinking, and a decent segment of your negative musings. For example, if you were approached to check the peas on your plate, it's your cognizant psyche that will add it up. The cognizant psyche also controls your deliberate activities, so when you choose to move your arms or legs, it's your cognizant brain advising you to complete the activity.

The intuitive piece of your psyche is liable for the entirety of your automatic activities. Your breathing and heartbeat are constrained by your subconscious. You don't need to consider it or advise your heart to pulsate; it's doing it all alone as programmed.

Consider it like driving a vehicle. At the point when you originally figured out how to drive, you needed to truly center and concentrate. Be that as it may, the more you do it, the more natural and agreeable you become out and about, and the less you needed to "think" about what you expected to do. It became programmed on the grounds that your intuition ingested how to drive on a cognizant level. You were being mindful of your subconscious information like, "A red light means stop. Green means go." Once we got capable at driving, we never again needed to intentionally process what we did when we went to a red light; our intuition dominated and our response was programmed. The information was put away in our subliminal memory, and again and again the information it stores can create tireless negative contemplations.

Positive musings happen normally when you expel the more profound underlying foundations of negative reasoning.

We instruct our subconscious all that it knows, which means we're continually feeding it with information and that doesn't simply mean the right method to drive a vehicle. It implies we feed it information that can likewise not be sure or beneficial to our prosperity. As it were, our musings are not as simple as what to do at a red light; that is, we may not really believe we're disclosing to ourselves things that aren't beneficial for us when we're thinking and handling contemplations that are discrediting or adverse, anything else than we would advise ourselves to speed through a red light. In any case, we accept our negative thoughts to be valid without testing them, we risk putting away them in our subconscious as our world, regardless of whether they are valid and genuine or not, can be compromising or risky to our prosperity as well.

Is there any valid reason why we wouldn't put a similar consideration we put into figuring out how to drive a vehicle as we do into what we let ourselves know? It's basic to challenge our negative thoughts when it springs up in our cognizant brain so we need to get them and challenge them before they get put away into our subconscious as convictions.

It's imperative to take note of that while the intuitive brain is the storm cellar/stockpiling zone for our musings, it is liable for the consequently activated sentiments and feelings that we experience after confronting every circumstance. Until we recognize what negative musings our cognizant psyche is telling our inner mind, we're not in charge of what we think we are, which can influence each choice we make, each longing we have, each objective, and we need to figure it out. Something other than encouraging our sentiments, which direct our activities, the cognizant and subconscious are our whole musings and are consolidated, which is quite an incredible mix.

CHAPTER 7
POWER OF POSITIVE THINKING

What Is Positive Thinking?

Positive thinking is a psychological and passionate demeanor that centers on the splendid side of life and anticipates positive outcomes.

An individual with positive reasoning mindset foresees satisfaction, health and achievement, and accepts that the individual in question can beat any hindrance and trouble.

Positive reasoning is not a school of thought that everybody sub-scribes to. A few thinks about it as drivel, and laugh at individuals who tail it. Be that as it may, there is a developing number of individuals who acknowledge positive speculation as a reality, and put stock in its viability.

It appears that this subject is picking up fame, as confirm by the nu-merous books, talks and courses about it.

To utilize it in your life, you need something to know about its reality. You have to embrace the disposition of positive intuition in all that you do.

How Positive Thinking Works

The accompanying story represents how positive reasoning func-tions.

Michael went after another position, yet he didn't accept he will get it, since his confidence was low, and he viewed himself as a disappointment and dishonorable of progress.

He had a negative demeanor toward himself, and along these lines, accepted that different candidates were preferred and progressively more qualified than him.

Michael's brain was busy with negative musings and fears concerning the activity for the entire week before going to the prospective employee meeting. He really had foreseen disappointment.

Upon the arrival of the meeting, he came late, and to his shock he found that the shirt he intended to wear was grimy, and the other one required pressing. As it was past the point of no return, he went out wearing a wrinkled shirt and without having breakfast.

During the meeting, he was tense, negative, ravenous, and stressed over his shirt. This occupied his brain and made it hard for him to concentrate on the meeting. His general conduct established an awful connection, and subsequently, he noticed his dread and didn't land the position.

Jerry went after a similar position as well, however, he moved toward the issue in an alternate manner. He was certain that he would land the position. During the week before going the meeting, he regularly pictured himself establishing a decent connection and landing the position.

In the night prior to the meeting, he arranged the garments he was going to wear, and rested. On day of the meeting, he woke up sooner than expected, and had abundant time to have breakfast and to show up to the meeting before the planned time.

Jerry established a decent connection and landed the position.

What do we gain from these two stories? Was there any enchantment utilized? No, everything occurred in a characteristic way.

Need to succeed in whatever You Do? THINK POSITIVE!

Positive reasoning is the best approach to progress.

Positive Thinking Is a Way of Life

With an inspirational demeanor we experience wonderful and cheerful sentiments. This carries brilliance to the eyes, more vitality, and satisfaction. Our entire being communicates positive attitude, joy, and achievement. Indeed, even our health is influenced in a helpful manner. We walk tall, our voice is more remarkable, and our non-verbal communication shows the manner in which we feel.

Positive and negative reasoning are infectious.

We influence, and are influenced by the individuals we meet. This happens instinctually and on a subconscious level through words, considerations and sentiments, and through non-verbal communication.

Is anyone surprised that we need to associate with constructive individuals and like to stay away from negative ones?

Individuals are arranged to support us—in the event that we are certain—and they despise and evade anybody broadcasting cynicism.

Negative musings, words and disposition, make negative and despondent emotions, states of mind, and conduct. At the point when the psyche is negative, harms are discharged into the blood, which causes more depression and pessimism. This is the best approach to disappointment, dissatisfaction, and frustration.

Can Positive Thinking Turn Out to Be Negative?

Research proposes cut-off points to looking on the radiant side of life.

"Highlight the positive," the 1944 tune by Johnny Mercer and Harold Arlen merrily entreated us. From Benjamin Franklin's 1750 Poor Richard's Almanac (which exhorted peruses that "distress is useless except however for sin") to the present procession of inspirational orator, Americans have since grasped a hopeful, "can-do" mentality toward life. Fitting "positive speculation" into Amazon.com, you will discover an endless stockpile of items intended to assist us with seeing life through rose-hued focal points, including an "Intensity of Positive Thinking" divider schedule and a "Beating Adversity with Encouragement and Affirmation" banner arrangement.

Actually, be that as it may, inspiration is not all it's made out to be. In spite of the fact that having a peppy demeanor without a doubt has its advantages, increases, for example, better health and riches from cheerful dispositions remain to a great extent undemonstrated. Look into recommends that confidence can be hindering in specific situations.

Positive Thinking Instructions and Advice

So, to turn the psyche towards the positive, some inward work is required since disposition and contemplations don't change medium-term.

- Find out about this subject, consider its advantages, and convince yourself to attempt it. The intensity of your contemplations is forceful and continually molds your life. This molding is generally done intuitively, yet it is conceivable to make the procedure a cognizant one. Regardless of whether the thought appears to be abnormal, check it out. You don't have anything to lose

- Overlook what others state or think about you, in the event that they find you are changing the manner you think.

- Utilize your creative mind to picture just ideal and useful circumstances

- Utilize positive words in your internal discoursed, or when conversing with others

- Grin somewhat more, as this assists with suspecting decisively

- When a negative idea enters your mind, you must know about it and try to supplant it with a productive one. In the event that the negative idea returns, supplant it again with a positive one.

- Diligence will in the long run show your brain to think emphatically and to overlook negative contemplations

- If you experience internal obstruction and troubles when supplanting negative contemplations with positive ones, don't surrender

- It doesn't make a difference what your conditions are. Think in a positive manner, anticipate great outcomes, circumstances, and conditions that will change. In the event that you endure, you will

change how your psyche thinks. It may require some investment
for the progressions to happen, however, in the end, they will

- Another valuable procedure is the reiteration of affirmations.
  This strategy is like inventive representation and can be utilized

Positive Thinking Words and Phrases

Include useful, idealistic, helpful, and urging words to your discussions. While thinking, endeavor to utilize such words as well, to drive away negative musings and negative words.

Right now, change your attitude from negative to positive, and your life will change in this manner.

Here Is a List of Words to Use:

Cheerful, Successful, Satisfied, Joy, Encouragement, Motivated, Agreeable, Attractive, Beautiful, Charming, Kind, Patient, Accomplish, Creative, Harmony, Inspirational, Constructive, Helpful.

Here Is a List of Phrases to Use:

- I feel better
- My life is continually improving
- I can
- I am capable
- Is conceivable
- It is within my grasp
- Everything will end up well
- I am a hopeful person
- I anticipate the best and give a valiant effort

- I esteem the good things in my life and thank the Universe for them
- I invite each day with affection and happiness
- I can and I will achieve my objectives

For additional Phrases read 35 Positive Thinking Phrases to Change Your Life.

Positive Thinking Quotes (paraphrased)

"Hardly any things on the planet are more remarkable than a positive push. A grin. A universe of positive thinking and expectation. A 'you can do it' when things are extreme."

- Richard M. Devos

"On the off chance that you have an uplifting demeanor and continually endeavor to give your best exertion, in the long run you will defeat your prompt issues and discover you are prepared for more prominent difficulties."

- Pat Riley

"Try not to be pushed around by the feelings of dread in your psyche. Be driven by the fantasies in your heart."

- Roy T. Bennett

"Any place you go, regardless of what the climate, continually bring your own daylight."

- Anthony J. D'Angelo

"Keep your fantasies alive. Comprehend to accomplish anything requires confidence and faith in yourself, vision, difficult work, assurance, and devotion. Recollect everything are workable for the individuals who accept."

- Gail Devers

"It's not the circumstance, however whether we respond negative or react positive to the circumstance that is significant."

- Zig Ziglar

"Embracing an extremely uplifting mentality can do some amazing things to adding a very long time to your life, a spring to your progression, a radiance to your eye, what not."

- Christie Brinkley

How to Think Positive Thoughts When Feeling Negative

Positive reasoning is an astonishing approach to keep your body, soul and mind in ideal conditions and would assist you with getting the best out of life.

Yet, life wasn't intended to be a bed of roses, so here and there, specific circumstances will come up that would make it difficult to keep an inspirational viewpoint. Find a way to cause positive deduction to turn out to be increasingly similar to your natural and you'll receive the greatest rewards.

Here Are 9 Different Ways to Make Thinking Positive Thinking Simple:

1. Invest Energy with Positive People

In the event you surround yourself with consistent grumblers, their cynicism is probably going to come off on you.

Invest energy with positive loved ones to improve the probability that their positive reasoning propensities will turn into yours as well. It's difficult to be negative when everybody around you is so optimistic.

2. Assume Liability for Your Actions

At the point when you experience issues and troubles throughout everyday life, don't assume the job of the person in question. Recognize your job in the circumstance and assume liability for your conduct.

Tolerating obligation can assist you with gaining from mistakes and keep you from accusing others unreasonably.

3. Add to the Community

Perhaps the most ideal approaches to like what you have is to concentrate on what you need to give.

Volunteer in some way and offer back to the network. Helping other people can give you another attitude toward the world and can help you with constructive reasoning.

4. Understand Positive and Inspirational Materials

Invest energy every day perusing something that energizes positive reasoning. Peruse the Bible, profound material, or uplifting statements to assist you with concentrating on what's essential to you throughout everyday life. It may very well be an extraordinary method to begin and end your day.

You won't be effective at positive reasoning despite everything tormented by visiting negative considerations. Figure out how to perceive and supplant thoughts that are excessively negative.

Frequently, contemplations that incorporate words like "consistently" and "never" signal that they aren't valid.

In the event that you end up speculating something, for example, "I consistently mess everything up," supplant it with something progressively reasonable like, "Once in a while I commit errors, however, I gain from them."

There's no compelling reason to make your contemplations ridiculously positive, however, make them increasingly sensible.

5. **Build up and Strive Toward Goals**

It's simpler to be certain about issues and misfortunes when you have objectives that you're moving in the direction of. Objectives will give you inspiration to conquer those deterrents when you experience issues. Without clear objectives, it's harder to settle on choices and check your advancement.

Figure out how to set SMART objectives (Specific, Measurable, Attainable, Relevant, Time-Based) to assist you with accomplishing more.

6. **Think About the Consequences of Negativity**

Invest some energy pondering the results of negative reasoning. Frequently, it can turn into an inevitable outcome.

For example, for an individual who thinks, "I most likely won't land this position," may invest less energy into the meeting. Subsequently, he may diminish his odds of landing the position.

Make a rundown of the considerable number of ways negative reasoning effects your life. It likely impacts your conduct, your connections, and your emotions. At that point, make a rundown of the manners by which positive reasoning could be advantageous.

7. Offer Compliments to Others

Search for motivations to praise others. Be authentic in your recognition and praises, yet offer it as often as possible. This will assist you with searching for the positive qualities in others.

8. Make a Daily Gratitude List

If you begin keeping a day by day appreciation list, you'll begin seeing the amount you must be grateful for. This can assist you with concentrating on the positive in your life as opposed to pondering all the terrible things that have occurred in the day.

Getting prone to show a disposition of appreciation makes positive thinking progressively about a propensity.

9. Practice Self-Mindfulness

Take great consideration of yourself and you'll be prepared to think decisively.

Get a lot of rest and exercise and work on dealing with your stress well. Dealing with your physical and mental health will give you more vitality to concentrate on positive reasoning.

The Power of the Placebo Effect

This is something many refer to as the "Misleading Impact." Know about it? Well if not, then plan to be enlightened. But regardless of whether you have, there's opportunity to get better. So, how's about we get to it.

Your brain can be a ground-breaking mending instrument whenever given the opportunity. The possibility that your brain can persuade your body a phony treatment is the genuine article — the supposed misleading impact — and accordingly animate recuperating has been around for centuries. Presently science has discovered that under the correct conditions, a fake treatment can be as successful as conventional medications.

"The placebo effect is more than positive reasoning — accepting a treatment or method will work. It's tied in with making a more grounded association between the mind and body and how they co-operate," says Professor Ted Kaptchuk of Harvard-subsidiary Beth Is-rael Deaconess Medical Center, whose examination centers around the misleading impact.

Fake treatments won't bring down your cholesterol or psychologist a tumor. Rather, fake treatments deal with side effects tweaked by the brain, similar to the view of agony. "Fake treatments may cause you to feel better, yet they won't fix you," says Kaptchuk. "They have been demonstrated to be best for conditions like agony the board, stress-related a sleeping disorder, and malignancy treatment reactions like weariness and sickness."

Does the Placebo Effect Mean Disappointment or Achievement?

For a considerable length of time, a Placebo effect was viewed as an indication of disappointment. A fake treatment is utilized in clinical preliminaries to test the adequacy of medicines and is regularly uti-lized in sedate examinations. For example, individuals in a single gath-ering got tried the medication, while the others got a phony medica-tion, or fake treatment, that they believed was the genuine article.

Along these lines, the specialists can quantify if the medication works by looking at how the two gatherings respond. In the event that the two of them had a similar response — improvement or not — the medication is considered not to work.

As of late, specialists have inferred that responding to a fake treatment can't be a specific treatment doesn't work, instead that another, a non-pharmacological system might be available.

How fake treatments work is yet to be seen, however, it includes a complex neurobiological response that remembers everything from increments for feel-good synapses, similar to endorphins and dopamine, and to more prominent action in certain mind areas connected to dispositions, enthusiastic responses, and mindfulness. Every last bit of it can have remedial advantage. "The Placebo effect is a path for your brain to mention to the body what it needs to feel much improved," says Kaptchuk.

In any case, fake treatments are not tied in with discharging mental ability. You also need the custom of treatment. "At the point when you take a look at these investigations that contrast medications and fake treatments, there is the whole natural and custom factor grinding away," says Kaptchuk. "You need to go to a facility at specific occasions and be inspected by clinical experts in white coats. You get a wide range of colorful pills and experience abnormal systems. This can profoundly affect how the body sees side effects since you believe you are getting consideration and care."

Give Yourself a Placebo?

Placebo treatments regularly work since individuals don't realize they're getting one. Yet, what occurs in the event that you realize you're getting a fake treatment?

A recent report drove by Kaptchuk and distributed in Science Translational Medicine investigated this by testing how individuals responded to a headache torment drug. One gathering took a headache sedate named with the medication's name, another took a fake treatment named "fake treatment," and a third gathering took nothing. The scientists found that the fake treatment was half as viable as the genuine medication to decrease torment after a headache assault.

The scientists hypothesized that a main thrust past this response was the straightforward demonstration of taking a pill. "Individuals partner the custom of accepting medication as a positive mending impact," says Kaptchuk. "Regardless of whether they know it's not medication, the activity itself can invigorate the mind into intuition the body is being mended."

How might you give yourself a fake treatment other than taking a phony pill? Rehearsing self-improvement strategies is one way. "Participating in the custom of sound living — eating right, working out, yoga, strength social time, reflecting — likely gives a portion of the key elements of a Placebo effect," says Kaptchuk.

While these exercises are sure intercessions in their own right, the degree of consideration you give can improve their advantages. "The consideration and enthusiastic help you give yourself is frequently not something you can undoubtedly gauge, yet it can assist you with feeling progressively good on the planet, and that can go far with regards to recuperating."

The Fake Treatment Sweet Spot

An investigation distributed online Oct. 27, 2016, by PLOS Biology may have recognized what goes on in the mind during a Placebo effect. Specialists utilized useful attractive reverberation imaging to examine the minds of individuals with ceaseless torment from knee osteoarthritis. At that point everybody was given a fake treatment and had another mind examine. The scientists saw that the individuals who felt relief from discomfort had more noteworthy action in the center frontal gyrus brain locale, which makes up around 33% of the frontal flap.

Idealism vs. an Inspirational Attitude

Idealism – Dangerous Positive Thinking

Idealism is accepting things will end up well, in any event, when the proof contends the opposite. The issue with this sort of positive reasoning is that it moves you away from the truth. Whenever you move away from reality of your circumstance, you'll settle on poor choices and get lousy outcomes.

Think about the accompanying instances of risky confidence:

1) Continuing to smoke, since you don't accept you'll get lung malignancy

2) Staying in a messed-up relationship since you trust it will mysteriously improve

3) Working an impasse work since you're wagering on an impossible advancement

4) Not putting something aside for your retirement since you accept you'll win the lottery

Clearly, in these cases, accepting beneficial things will happen is going to shield you from making enhancements in your life. Unfounded good faith is hazardous.

In spite of these models, numerous individuals (and numerous creators) have contended that there are advantages to trick yourself into accepting impossible, beneficial things will happen. This has made a great deal of disarray towards positive intuition and, as I would see it, a significant part of the criticism towards the self-improvement development.

Regularly expressed models are:

1) Believing in yourself when nobody else does, can push you to achieve large things

2) Optimism can assist you with remaining focused on an objective when there is no outside support

3) Faith in your activities can assist you with bouncing back from demoralizing disappointments

In these cases, I'll concur, good faith can be helpful. The issue is that it's difficult to unmistakably isolate the instances of truly supportive positive thinking from perilous optimism. An untruth is a falsehood, regardless of how you turn it.

A superior point of view to receive is one that stays consistent with your circumstance, yet in addition gives you the inspiration you have to work hard. Here are a couple of viewpoints to consider that are straightforward, yet in addition urge you to continue onward:

It's smarter to attempt to fall flat, at that point not to try. Helen Keller has an extraordinary statement that outlines the choice we as a whole face splendidly, "Life is either a challenging experience or nothing. To keep our countenances toward change and act like free spirits within the sight of destiny is strength undefeatable."

We gain from disappointments, not from success. Continuing after a disappointment doesn't require idealism, on the grounds that each blunder expands on your knowledge. Each error carries you closer to progress.

The reason for having objectives is roused action. Setting objectives isn't about accomplishment, it's tied in with getting you to feel enlivened and take action. Even if achievement isn't anticipated, you realize your objective has fulfilled its need.

These are only a couple of viewpoints, yet there are innumerable others. The fact of the matter is that you shouldn't have to deceive yourself so as to remain motivated. Realistically seeing the circumstance should push you to make the best decisions. The explanation this happens is the point where you develop a truly great type of positive reasoning.

Inspirational Attitude, the Useful Positive Thinking

Idealism is contemplating the things that will happen. An inspirational demeanor is tied in with being certain of the things you consider. Unlike good faith, an uplifting disposition doesn't welcome falsehoods. It doesn't ask that you give up your thinking capacities to make decisions. Because an inspirational mentality lines up with reality of your existence, you can be as positive as you like without the risks of presumptuousness or pomposity.

So as to clarify the contrast among demeanor and confidence, I'll utilize an example. Let's say you're unhealthy. Although this may appear to be a chilly certainty, there are extremely numerous ways you can speak to yourself inside:

- I'm going to kick the bucket
- I'm an undesirable individual
- I have an issue with diet and exercise
- I have habits I need to work on
- I have a test and a chance to increase the quality of my life

These are true. You can't take a look at any of those pronouncements and can't help contradicting it in case you're out of shape. However, your mind can't think with those examples simultaneously. You can just think one point of view at a time. An uplifting disposition is tied in with developing the viewpoints that are the most valuable for creating change.

Good faith would include beguiling yourself about the results. You would know you weren't going to endure your unforeseen weakness or that you weren't generally unhealthy. You may also accept that changing your health would be simple (and rapidly surrender when it gets too hard). An uplifting disposition doesn't make that blunder.

Step by Step Guide to Thinking Positively

Having an uplifting standpoint is a decision. You can decide to think contemplations that hoist your temperament, toss an increasingly helpful light on troublesome circumstances, and for the most part, shading your day with more splendid, confident ways to deal with the things you do. By deciding to take an uplifting point of view, you can start to move out of a negative outlook and consider life to be loaded up with potential outcomes and arrangements rather than stresses and snags. In the event that you need to realize how to think decisively, simply follow these tips.

1. Take Duty Regarding Your Mentality

You are liable for your thoughts and your point of view is a choice. If you will think you are deciding to believe that way. With training, you can decide to have a progressively positive outlook.

2. Understand the Advantages of Being a Positive Thinker

Deciding to think decisively won't just assist you with assuming responsibility for your life and make your regular encounters progressively charming, however, it can profit your psychological and physical health just as your capacity to manage change. Monitoring these advantages can enable you to be persuaded to think emphatically on a normal basis. Here are a few advantages of positive reasoning:

- An expanded life expectancy
- Lower paces of hypochondria and depression
- More prominent protection from the basic virus
- Better mental and physical prosperity
- Better adapting abilities during times of stress
- A common capacity to frame connections and form bonds

3. Keep a Journal to Mirror Your Contemplations

Recording your contemplations can empower you to step back and assess designs in your reasoning. Record your musings and emotions and attempt to detect any triggers that lead to positive or negative contemplations. Taking twenty minutes to follow your example of deduction toward the finish of consistently can be a significant method to distinguish your negative musings and to make an arrangement to transform them into positive considerations.

Your diary can take on any structure that you like. In the event that you couldn't care to compose wordy intelligent passages, you can simply make a rundown of the five most pervasive negative musings and positive considerations you had that day.

Make certain to give yourself the time and chance to assess and consider the information in the diary. If you compose each day, you might need to reflect toward the finish.

How might you pinpoint your negative examples of thought so you can begin moving to progressively positive reasoning?

- Talk with a companion
- A diary
- Care
- Assume liability for your contemplations

Battling Negative Thoughts

1. Identify Your Programmed Negative Contemplations

To move away from the negative reasoning that is keeping you away from having an uplifting standpoint, you'll have to turn out to be mindful of your "programmed negative contemplations." At the point when you remember them, you're in a situation to challenge them and provide them their walking requests to move directly out of your head.

A case of a programmed negative idea is, after hearing that you have an up and coming test, you think, "I'll likely flunk it." The idea is programmed in light of the fact that it's your underlying response to catching wind of the test.

2. Challenge Your Negative Considerations

Regardless of whether you have consumed a large portion of your time on earth thinking contrarily, you don't need to keep being negative. At whatever point you have a negative idea, especially a programmed negative idea, stop and assess whether the idea is valid or accurate.

One approach to challenge negative contemplations is to be objective. Record the negative idea and consider how you would react if another person said the idea to you. Almost certainly, you could offer a rejoinder to another person's cynicism, regardless of what you think is hard to accomplish for yourself.

For instance, you may have the negative idea, "I generally flunk tests." It is impossible that you would in any case be in school in the event that you generally bombed tests. Revisit your records or evaluations and discover tests that you got a passing evaluation on; these test the negative idea. You may even find that you have tests that you went with, which would affirm that your pessimism is misrepresented.

3. Replace the Negative Considerations with Positive Contemplations

When you're feeling certain that you can spot and challenge negative considerations, you're prepared to settle on dynamic decisions about supplanting negative contemplations with positive ones. This doesn't imply that everything in your life will consistently be certain; it's not unexpected to have an assortment of feelings. Notwithstanding, you can work to supplanting the everyday unhelpful speculation designs with musings that help you to thrive.

For instance, in the event that you have the idea, "I will most likely bomb the test," stop yourself. You've just recognized the idea as negative and assessed its precision. Take a stab at supplanting it with a positive idea. A positive idea doesn't need to be aimlessly idealistic, for example, "I will get a 100 on the test, regardless of whether I don't contemplate." It can be something as straightforward as, "I am going to set aside effort to consider and plan so I excel on the test as I can."

Utilize the intensity of inquiries. At the point when you ask your mind an inquiry, it will discover the response for you. If you ask yourself, "For what reason is life so horrible?" your mind will attempt to respond to your inquiry. The equivalent is valid if you ask yourself, "How could I get the chance to be so fortunate?" Ask yourself inquiries which draw your center onto positive musings.

4. Minimize Outside Impacts That Invigorate Your Pessimism

You may know that particular sorts of music, fierce computer games, or motion pictures impact your general attitude. Try limiting your introduction to distress and invest more energy tuning in to quieting music or perusing. Music benefits your brain truly well and books on constructive reasoning can give great tips to being a more joyful individual.

5. Avoid "High Contrast Thinking"

Thinking, otherwise called "polarizing," is all that you experience either it is or it isn't; there are no shades of dim. This can lead individuals to feel just as they need to accomplish something impeccably or not at all.

To maintain a strategic distance from this sort of reasoning, grasp the shades of darkness throughout everyday life. Rather than intuition as far as two results (one positive and one negative), make a rundown of the entirety of the results in the middle to see that things aren't as critical as they appear.

For instance, if you have a test coming up and don't feel good with the topic, you might be tempted to not go for the exam or to not read for it by any means, so in the event that you fizzle, this is on the grounds that you didn't attempt. In any case, this is disregarding the way that you're probably going to improve in the event that you invest more energy getting ready for the test.

6. Avoid "Personalizing"

Personalizing is making the suspicion that you are at fault for whatever turns out badly. If you take this kind of speculation excessively far, you can get suspicious and feel that nobody likes you or needs to spend time with you, and that each and every move you make will baffle someone.

Somebody who is personalizing may think, "Betty didn't grin at me toward the beginning of today. I probably did something to upset her." However, almost certainly, Betty was simply having an awful day, and her mind-set had nothing to do with you.

7. Abstain From "Filter Thinking"

This is the point where you decide to hear the negative side of a circumstance. Most circumstances have components that are both acceptable and awful, and it assists with perceiving both. If you think along these lines, at that point you'll never observe the positive in any situation.

For instance, you may step through an exam and get a C, alongside the input from your educator saying that your exhibition improved extraordinarily from the last test. Separating this can make you ponder the C and overlook the way that you have demonstrated improvement and development.

8. Avoid "Catastrophizing"

This is the point where you accept that the most exceedingly awful and conceivable result is going to happen. Catastrophizing is typically identified with anxiety about performing inadequately. You can battle catastrophizing with being reasonable about potential results of a circumstance.

For instance, you may feel that you will bomb a test you've been reading for. A catastrophize will at that point stretch out that weakness to expect that you'll bomb the class and need to drop out of school, and become jobless and on government assistance. In case you're practical about negative results, you'll understand that regardless of whether you were to bomb a test, it's improbable that you would essentially bomb the course, and you would not need to drop out of school.

9. Visit a Quiet Spot

It can assist with having an individual departure when you have to turn your disposition around. Numerous individuals find that investing a little energy outside improves their mood.

If your working environment has an open-air region with seats or outdoor tables, plan yourself a little personal time to be outside and revive yourself.

If you can't genuinely visit an outside serene spot, have a go at ruminating and visiting a wonderful open-air region with ideal climate in your mind.

What is a case of catastrophizing?

- "She didn't snicker at my joke, so I may not be clever."
- "I'm either going to get a top review or flunk this test."
- "In the event that I bomb this test, I will flop out of school."

Carrying on With an Optimistic Life

1. **Give Yourself an Opportunity to Change**

Building up an uplifting standpoint is really the improvement of an expertise. Likewise, with any expertise, it sets aside some effort to ace, and it requires committed practice and delicate updates about not falling go into negative thinking.

2. **Be Genuinely Positive**

In the event that you change your physical or real propensities, your psyche will take action accordingly. So, to feel more joyful as a rule, approach your genuineness in a positive way. Practice having a great stance, standing upright and holding your shoulders down and back. A droop will cause you to feel increasingly negative. Grin more frequently. Not only will others grin back at you, the demonstration of grinning may persuade your body that you are happier.

3. Practice Care

Being increasingly mindful of your activities and your life will cause you to feel more joyful. At the point when you basically make a half-hearted effort of your life like a robot, you will probably neglect to discover the delight in ordinary things. By being careful about your environment, your decisions, and your day by day exercises, you can oversee your life and your happiness.

Think about taking up reflection as an approach to focus yourself and learn superb core interest. By contemplating each day for ten to twenty minutes during a period that is advantageous for you, you can build your attention to yourself and the present, helping you to corral the thinking with a more prominent consciousness.

Have a go at taking a yoga class. Yoga can assist you with getting increasingly mindful of the world as you connect with your breathing.

Indeed, even simply halting to take full breaths and rest your brain for a couple of seconds can cause you to feel more joyful.

4. Investigate Your Inventive Side

If you haven't got an opportunity to investigate your innovative side right now, setting aside the effort to be aesthetic and to work with your hands or investigate your most unique musings can do wonders for your capacity to consider new ideas and to think positively. Even in the event that you don't believe you're normally disposed toward imagination, there are various ways you can communicate to turn out to be more positive.

- Take a class to find out about something you've never done: think about ceramics, painting, blended media montage, verse, or wood working

- Take a stab at learning another art, for example, weaving, stitching, sewing, or needlepoint. Specialty stores and online instructional exercises are incredible assets for learners who would prefer not to take a class

- Doodle in a sketchbook. Take a stab at returning to more seasoned drawings and transforming them into something new

- Be an innovative essayist. Take a stab at writing a sonnet, short story, or even take a stab at a novel. You can even play out your verse at an open mic night

- Attempt pretending, dressing as your preferred TV or comic book character, or going for a section at a network theatre

5. **Surround Yourself with Constructive Individuals**

We are frequently impacted by the individuals around us. If encircle yourself with progressively constructive people. This will take mindfulness of your own inspiration. If you have a nearby relative or someone who is continually negative, urge them to go on an excursion towards energy with you.

Evade individuals who sap your vitality and inspiration. In the event that you can't stay away from them, or would prefer not to, figure out how not to let them get you down and keep your association with them brief.

Abstain from dating anybody with a negative standpoint. In case you're inclined to negative reasoning, you'll be falling into a snare. In the event that you do end up involved with somebody who battles to think emphatically, however, looking for directing together may be your best choice.

6. **Set Significant Objectives**

Whatever your objective might be, you should keep yourself occupied with dealing with it and trust the reason you've set for yourself. When you arrive at the main objective, you will be roused to proceed with the rest of the objectives, just by adding new ones to your life. With every objective you accomplish, regardless of how little, you will pick up certainty and your confidence will expand, taking mindfulness of greater energy in your life.

Moving in the direction of accomplishing your objectives regardless of whether you're simply making little strides, can cause you to feel happier.

7. **Don't Neglect to Have Some Good Times**

Individuals who permit themselves standard enjoyment in their lives will be more joyful and progressively positive since it isn't all drudgery and endless dreariness. Fun separates the difficult work and difficulties. Recall that fun doesn't appear to be identical for everybody, so you may need to invest energy finding a movement that is a good time for you.

Continuously set aside a few minutes for chuckling. Spend time with companions who make you giggle, go to a parody club, or watch an entertaining film. It'll be difficult to think adversely when your entertaining bone is being tickled.

Tips for Maintaining a Positive Attitude

Keeping up an inspirational disposition is basic when you need to accomplish anything ... or just to improve an incredible nature. So, note that realizing how to think decisively is only one significant bit of the puzzle, another is really realizing how to keep up your energy.

Right now, discover 11 hints for keeping up your uplifting mentality regardless of what's happening in your life.

1. You Determine Your Reality

Realize that you decide your existence by how you respond to the outside world. When something occurs, you get the opportunity to pick whether it's a positive or negative understanding and respond as need be. Losing your employment may be a debacle or it may be the open door for greater and more splendid things ... you pick what it will intend for you.

2. Start Your Day Strong

The greater part of the populace needs to drag themselves up and this sets a negative edge for their whole day. Constructive individuals make a wake-up routine that strengthens how incredible life is and that they are so glad to be alive.

I used to wake up and promptly turn on Bon Jovi's "It's My Life" to get me into gear. I start my day by perusing or tuning in to something positive. Regardless of whether you have one moment, fifteen minutes or an hour to commit to your custom, you can begin the day in whatever state you like.

3. **Exercise Is the Natural Feel-Good Drug**

Exercise is an extraordinary method to keep up a decent mentality on account of all the positive synthetic substances it discharges into the circulation system. I used to practice in the first part of the day (after Bon Jovi) and this is regularly prescribed as an amazing method. I practice by doing exercises I love (Kung Fu and choreography) most nights, however, even a stroll around the square with motivating sound will help.

4. **Use Books, Audio and Videos to Overload Your Brain with Positivity**

There are a huge number of stunning books, digital recordings, and recordings for you to assimilate from individuals who are carrying on with the life they have always wanted. Tap into their positive feelings and their experience by figuring out how they think and what they do to make the lives they need.

You can do this toward the beginning of the day or while working out, eating, driving, cooking, cleaning ... there's consistently time for inspiration.

5. **Your Language Shapes Your Thoughts**

Little changes in your language can change the manner where you think and how you act. At whatever point somebody welcomes you and asks how you're doing; do you answer with "fine" or "not all that terrible?" think about what this language is conveying to other people ... and to yourself.

I answer with "extraordinary," "phenomenal," or "astounding." Not only does this advise me that life truly is incredible, it typically amazes and lifts the condition of the individual I'm conversing with.

6. Spend Time with Positive People

It is frequently said that you will have a comparable degree of health, salary and way of life as the five individuals you invest the most energy with: The Hidden Power of Every Single Person Around You.

So, if you need to be fit, begin to spend time with fit individuals. Need to begin a business? At that point spend time with entrepreneurs. Furthermore, if you need to be sure, spend time with constructive individuals.

7. Show Your Appreciation for Others

By acknowledging others for an occupation, their outfit or their grin, you begin to cause a positive chain response.

Don't you feel extraordinary when you get a commendation from another person? Indeed, if you need to get, at that point begin giving them out and watch what befalls the individuals around you.

8. Trash In, Garbage Out

This is an articulation from programming where the outcome is just on par with the information. So, if you're taking mindfulness of yourself with cynicism throughout the day, at that point it's entirely evident you will feel negative too.

A great deal of the media including news and TV blossom with pessimism. So, put yourself on a cynicism diet (counting individuals) and watch how much simpler it is to keep up your inspirational disposition.

9. Leave Negative Thoughts Speechless

It's difficult to be a continually constructive individual and negative considerations are going to rise every now and again. These will come and go as you practice the tips we're discussing. At the point when you begin to see negative contemplations, you can utilize an example hinder to leave them speechless.

The thought is to interfere with your present idea example and change your state. My best one is The Smurfs signature tune. At whatever point I begin to feel disappointed, miserable or irate I begin murmuring the tune and a major senseless grin comes over my face.

10. Live with Gratitude

Such a large number of positive things occur during our day and we frequently overlook them while allowing one negative or occasion to ruin our disposition. It can assist with keeping an appreciation diary where you write down things you are thankful for every night or during the day.

If you're understanding this, at that point you live with a rooftop over your head and have nourishment in your stomach, which is an everyday battle for a large portion of the world ... so it ought to be anything but difficult to track down huge amounts of things you're thankful for.

11. Revive Your Batteries

A vital aspect for keeping up your inspirational demeanor is setting aside the effort to energize your batteries. This may mean taking a couple hours toward the end of the week to peruse a positive book or taking half a month for a vacation.

In case you're not in the situation to travel, you can take a staycation, or have a "home occasion" where you basically switch off from the outside world and invest energy doing things you love.

Last Thoughts

You currently have eleven hints for keeping up your uplifting disposition, yet they are no utilization to you except if you actualize them into your life.

Start little. Pick the most effortless tip or the one that you truly adore and bring it into your life beginning at the present time. At that point after some time, begin actualizing different tips and watch your energy take off.

CHAPTER 8
TAKING BACK YOUR MIND

Knowing your enemy is only half of the battle. Now it's time to get your hands dirty and take back control. Here are some sure proven strategies to help you do that.

1. Act "as though"

It's a characteristic propensity to act as per our emotions. Subsequently, it very well may be enticing to hold up until you feel distinctive to roll out an improvement.

However, putting off applying for an advancement until you feel sure, you'll get your accounts all together when you feel less overpowered and aren't acceptable to methodologies.

Rather, studies show you ought to act like the individual you need to turn into. Make a move first and you'll change the manner in which you think and the manner in which you feel.

Here's a model. At the point when you feel dismal, you're probably going to hunch your shoulders, avoid eye to eye contact, and partake less in discussions. Those practices keep you in a burdensome state.

In any case, if you grinned, set your shoulders back, and begin some well-disposed discussion. You'll feel an instant spike in your mood.

So, don't anticipate that your feelings should mysteriously change. Make a move and get it going. When you're feeling unreliable, ask yourself, how might I act sure? Acting sure will diminish your self-question.

So, whenever you're feeling stuck, ask yourself what might an intellectually resilient individual do? At that point, go about as though you feel solid as of now.

2. Practice Mindfulness

Repeating something that happened yesterday or anticipating horrendous things could occur one week from now will keep you down. The main time you can change your conduct is at the present time, so it's critical to have the option to concentrate on the present time and place.

A large number of studies have discovered mindfulness gives physical and mental advantages. Decreased stress and a progressively compassionate internal exchange are among the numerous way mindfulness can assist you with building mental strength.

So, pause for a moment to focus on what's happening around you. Notice the sounds, sights, and scents. Do a snappy scan of your body and focus on how it feels.

With ordinary practice, you'll increment your capacity to focus, which is hard to do in the present uproarious world. You'll also have the option to appreciate every minute when you're not diverted by yesterday's issues and tomorrow's stresses.

3. Distinguish Three Things You're Thankful For

Considering your gifts — contradicted to your weights — quickly improves mental health. Studies show appreciation expands bliss and lessens hypochondria.

Make appreciation an everyday propensity by recognizing three things you are grateful for. Your appreciation rundown could be as basic as feeling grateful for the clean water that runs out of your kitchen sink or valuing the warm sun on a cool day.

Studies show your mind will truly change when you make appreciation a propensity. After some time, being grateful becomes like natural and you'll encounter benefits going from improved rest to better invulnerability.

4. Do Your Mental Push Ups

Each day is a chance to build more mental muscle. Straightforward, short activities will assist you with building mental strength.

Moreover, focus on the negative behavior patterns that deny you of mental strength. Feeling frustrated about yourself, parting with your capacity, and detesting others' prosperity are only a couple of the negative behavior patterns that could unleash destruction on your psychological exercises. Surrendering those undesirable propensities will assist you with working more efficiently.

5. Put Things into a More Extensive Perspective

It's exceptionally simple to fall into the snare of overthinking minor things throughout everyday life.

So, when you are considering something ask yourself: will this issue end in five years? Or, on the other hand, even in five weeks?

I've discovered that extending the point of view by utilizing this basic inquiry can rapidly wake me up from overthinking and help me to relinquish that circumstance.

It permits me to at long last quit pondering something and to concentrate my time and vitality on something different that really does make a difference.

6. Set Brief Time Frame Limits for Choices

If you don't have a period limit for when you should settle on a choice and make a move, then you can simply continue turn your thoughts around and see them from all points in your brain for an exceptionally prolonged stretch of time.

So, figure out how to be better at settling on choices and to get a move on setting cut-off times in your day by day life, regardless of if it's a little or greater choice.

This is what has worked for me:

For little choices like if ought to proceed to do the dishes, react to an email, or work out, I use a rule to allow myself thirty seconds or less to settle on a choice.

For fairly bigger choices that would have taken me days or weeks to thoroughly consider in the past, I utilize a cut-off time for thirty minutes to the finish the workday.

7. Quit Setting Your Day Up for Stress and Overthinking

You can't absolutely abstain from overpowering or having extremely upsetting days.

Yet, you can limit the quantity of them in your month and year by getting a decent beginning to your day and by not setting yourself up for pointless stress, overthinking, and languishing.

Three things that helped me with that are:

I. Get a Decent Beginning

I've referenced to this multiple occasion. What's more, in light of current circumstances?

How you start your day will regularly set the pace for your day.

A stressed morning will most likely result in a stressed day. Devouring negative information as you ride the transport to your job will lead to progressively critical contemplations during the remainder of your day.

While perusing something over breakfast, getting some activity and afterward begins with your most significant errand right establishes a decent pace for the afternoon and will assist you with staying positive.

II. Single-Undertaking and Take Ordinary Breaks

This will assist you with keeping a sharp concentration during your day and to complete what's generally significant while permitting you to rest and revive so you don't begin to barely get by.

What's more, this to some degree loosened up your outlook, yet with the restricted center, will assist you with thinking conclusively and abstain from ending up in a focused and overthinking head space.

III. Limit Your Day by Day Input

An excess of information, too often of simply taking a couple of moments to check your inbox, Facebook or Twitter record, or how your blog or site is doing, prompts more info and mess in your minds as your day advances.

Thus, it gets more diligently to think in a basic and clear manner and simpler to slip by once more into that overthinking propensity.

8. Action Speaks Louder Than Thoughts

At the point when you realize how to begin with making a move reliably every day, then you'll hesitate less by overthinking.

Setting cut-off times and a decent tone for the day are two things that have helped me to turn out to be considerably more of an individual of activity.

Making little strides forward and just concentrating on completing each little stride in turn is another propensity that has truly worked well.

It works so well since you don't feel overpowered thus you don't need to escape into lingering or sluggish inaction.

Furthermore, despite the fact you might be apprehensive, making only a stride is such a little thing, that you don't get incapacitated in dread.

9. Understand That You Can't Control Everything

Attempting to thoroughly consider things multiple times can be an approach to attempt to control everything. To cover each consequence so you don't by chance commit an error, fail, or look dumb.

Be that as it may, those things are a piece of carrying on with a real existence where you genuinely stretch your customary range of familiarity. Everybody who you may appreciate and have carried on with a real existence that moves you has fizzled. They have committed errors.

Yet, much of the time they've considered these to be a significant input to gain from.

Those things may look negative and have shown them a ton that have been important to assist them with growing.

So quit attempting to control everything. Attempting to do so just doesn't work. Nobody can see every single imaginable situation ahead of time.

This is obviously quite difficult. You can choose to take your time.

10. Say Stop in a Circumstance Where You Realize You Can't Think Straight

Here and there when I'm ravenous or when I'm lying in bed and I'm going to rest, negative thoughts begin humming around in my brain.

In the past they could do a lot of harm. These days I've gotten the hang of getting them and I state to myself:

"No, no, we won't dwell on this now."

I realize that when I'm eager or lethargic, then my mind will be helpless against not thinking obviously and to antagonism.

So, I follow up my "no, no ..." expression and I state to myself that I will thoroughly consider this circumstance or issue when I realize that my brain will work much better.

It took a touch of training to get this to work yet I've gotten quite great at deferring thinking right now. What's more, I know for a fact that when I return to a circumstance with some prudent speculation then in 80% of the cases the issue is extremely little to non-existent.

What's more, in the event that there is a main problem, at that point my mind is set up to manage it in much better and helpful manner.

11. Try Not to Lose All Sense of Direction in Obscure Feelings of Trepidation

Another snare I've fallen into that has prodded my overthinking is that I've become mixed up in ambiguous feelings of dread about a circumstance in my life.

Thus, my brain going out of control has made debacle situations about what could occur in the event that I accomplish something.

So, I've figured out how to ask myself: truly, what is the most terrible that could occur?

What's more, when I've made sense of what the most terrible thing that could happen really is then I can invest a little energy to think about what I can do if that regularly quite far-fetched thing occurs.

I've discovered the most terrible thing that could practically happen is normally something that can't, which is terrifying as to what my mind going out of control with obscure dread could deliver.

Discovering lucidity takes a couple of moments and bit of vitality, but it can spare you a ton of time and languishing.

12. **Work Out**

This may sound somewhat odd.

In any case, working out can truly help with relinquishing internal stress.

It causes me to feel progressively definitive and when I was a greater amount of an over thinker then, it was frequently my go-to strategy for changing the head space I was in to an increasingly valuable one.

13. **Get a Lot of Good Strength Rest**

I think this is one of the most ordinarily disregarded components with regards to keeping an inspirational mentality and not becoming mixed up in negative idea propensities.

When you haven't dozed enough then you become progressively powerless.

Powerless against stressing and negativity. To not think as obviously as you generally do. What's more, to getting lost in musings moving around and around in your mind as you overthink.

So, let me share a few my preferred tips that help me to rest better:

- Keep it cool

It can feel decent from the start to get into a comfortable room. However, I've discovered that I rest better and more serenely with less frightening or negative dreams in the event that I keep the room cool.

- Keep earplugs close by

If you, similar to me, are effortlessly awoken by clamors, then a couple straightforward earplugs can be a lifeline.

These modest things have helped me to get a decent night's rest through snorers, uproarious felines.

- Try not to attempt to drive yourself to rest

If you don't feel drowsy, at that point don't get into bed and attempt to compel yourself to rest.

That, in any event as far as I can tell, just prompts hurling and turning in my bed for an hour or more.

A superior arrangement in these circumstances is to slow down for an additional twenty to thirty minutes on the love seat with, for instance, some perusing. This causes me to rest quicker and, at last, get more rest.

14. Invest a Greater Amount of Your Energy Right Now

By being in your regular day to day existence as opposed to before or a potential future in your mind, you can supplant increasingly more of the time you have for the most part and go through on overthinking things with simply being here right now.

Three different ways that I frequently use to reconnect:

I. Slow down:

Slow down how you do whatever you are doing well at this point. Move slower, talk slower or ride your bike all the more gradually for instance.

By doing so you become progressively mindful of how you utilize your body and what's going on surrounding you at the present time.

ii Tell yourself: Now I am …

I frequently disclose this to myself: Now I am X. Also, X could be brushing my teeth. Going for a stroll in the forested areas. Or, on the other hand, doing the dishes.

This straightforward update causes my brain to quit meandering and takes my concentration back to what's going on at this time.

iii. Upset and reconnect:

If you believe you are becoming mixed up in overthinking or upset that idea by – in your brain – yell this to yourself: STOP!

At that point reconnect with the current minute by taking only one to two minutes to concentrate on what is happening around you. Take it all in with every one of your faculties. Feel it, hear it, smell it, see it, and sense it on your skin.

15. **Invest a Greater Amount of Your Energy with Individuals who Don't Overthink**

Your social condition has a major influence.

Furthermore, not simply the individuals and gatherings near you, all things considered. Yet in addition what you read, tune in to and watch. The web journals, books, gatherings, motion pictures, digital recordings and music in your life.

So, consider if there are any sources throughout your life – close by or far away – that energizes and tends make more overthinking in your brain. What's more, think about what individuals or sources have impact on you.

Discover approaches to invest a greater amount of your energy and consideration with the individuals and information that positively affect your reasoning and less on the impacts that will reinforce your overthinking propensity.

16. **Know about the issue (remind yourself throughout the day)**

Monitoring your test is imperative to bring an end to the propensity for overthinking.

In any case you're imagining that you'll simply make sure to quit overthinking during your ordinary day, at that point you're simply tricking yourself.

Two different sorts of updates that you can utilize are:

- A little composed note

Utilize post-it notes or something comparable and record my whiteboard expression with an inquiry like, "Am I over complicating this?" or some other update that interests you.

Put that note where you can't abstain from seeing it like, for instance, on your bedside table. Your restroom reflects next to your PC screen.

- Update on your smart mobile phone

Record one of the expressions above or one of you claim picking in an update application on your PDA.

I, for instance, utilize my Android telephone and the free application called Google Keep to do this.

CONCLUSION

We've finally come to the end of our journey. I hope everything you've learnt will prove to be a useful asset in taking back control of your mind and finally defeating the foe called "Overthinking."

Remember, practice makes perfect!

See you next time,

Emma

www.ingramcontent.com/pod-product-compliance
Lightning Source LLC
Chambersburg PA
CBHW031058250726
48655CB00004B/1492